ORIGINAL SURVEY AND LAND SUBDIVISION

ORIGINAL SURVEY AND LAND SUBDIVISION

A Comparative Study of the Form and Effect of Contrasting Cadastral Surveys

NORMAN J. W. THROWER

Fourth in the Monograph Series
Published for
The Association of American Geographers
by
Rand McNally & Company
Chicago

The Monograph Series of the
Association of American Geographers

EDITOR'S NOTE

PROFESSOR THROWER'S MONOGRAPH is one of a growing number of studies about an ancient and basic phenomenon, the way in which men have divided up their land, whether this subdivision has been irregular and haphazard, to all appearances without reason, or whether it reveals a devotion to geometry worthy of Euclid himself. Over most of the earth's surface and throughout most of human history, the first of these ways has been the most common. In many cases the pattern has survived in the visible appearance of the land, but the old sturdy oak or the large isolated rock, thought of in a bygone age as permanent, enduring, and setting the boundaries of land in perpetuity, may have disappeared. The surviving irregular shapes and aimless-appearing subdivisions give the impression of more irrationality in their making than may be justified historically.

Thrower compares the effects of two ways of dividing the land in an area of Northwestern Ohio, a reasonably homogeneous environment in all respects save the manner in which lines were drawn on the land at the beginning of European settlement. One was subdivided in an "unsystematic" manner, a term which the author uses in place of older designations of subdivisions by "metes and bounds" or "indiscriminate location," the other according to the American Rectangular Land Survey System.

This work has many counterparts in European studies of field systems. Vivid illustrations come from the history of the English enclosure movement, for the enclosures not only changed the use, but drastically altered the appearance of the land. Equally striking is the widespread occurrence of Roman centuriation, which has been studied in recent years by such scholars as Bradford, Kish (see bibliography), and Chevallier (*Études rurales,* Sommaire No. 3, Oct-Dec, 1961), and others. That different ways of subdividing land have influenced road patterns, settlements, methods of cultivation, taxation, litigation, even personal comfort and attitudes to the environment, is clear enough; the excitement comes with the detailed analysis whose possibilities are so well illustrated in this work. The text, graphs, and maps perform their assigned tasks well; the result is a scholarly study which carries conviction.

Although I must resist the temptation to compare Roman centuriation with the American Rectangular Land Survey System, it may be said that the American example is even more dramatic than the Roman despite the survivals in the Po Valley, in Apulia, in Tunis and other parts of North Africa. In the United States the division was of continental proportions and continuous mile after mile. Anyone who has flown over the United States on a clear day or who has studied detailed road maps of the country which show more than federal and state highways is aware of its influence, but in my experience the sight has been much more striking, dramatic, and worthy of study to foreigners than to Americans. Indeed, this observation applies to Thrower who was born in England where schoolboys grow up studying field systems. It is not surprising that this work, the first to my knowledge to make a detailed comparison of the effects of contrasting cadastral systems in the United States in the tradition of European study of field systems, enclosures, and centuriation, has come from the pen of an English scholar.

In this country, the doctoral dissertation of William Pattison revived interest in the American Rectangular Land Survey System; he however was concerned primarily with its history. Actually, Thrower's and Pattison's studies on different aspects of land subdivision developed contemporaneously, and independently, in the middle 1950's. (Norman J. W. Thrower, "Cadastral Survey and Roads in Ohio," in "Abstracts of Papers presented at the 53rd Annual Meeting of the Association of American Geographers, Cincinnati, Ohio, April 1-4, 1957," *Annals of the Association of American Geographers,* Vol. 47, No. 2, June, 1957, pp. 181-182, and in the same journal, issue, and section, p. 174, William D. Pattison, "The Original Plan Behind the Rectangular Subdivision of Land in the Old Northwest.") And Hildegard Binder Johnson has studied the rectangular subdivision, showing how the strong hand of geometry, persisting in property ownership and political subdivisions, is spread over many kinds of ecosystems. These works supplement one another well.

The painstaking way in which Thrower has studied these two areas and the comparisons he has made reveal promising areas of research in historical and cultural geography. His work is not only interesting in its own right; it is also methodologically interesting. The two charming lithographs (See Figures 35a and 35b), one farm with its severe geometry, the other with its graceful curves, tell their own story. They admirably illustrate the concluding paragraphs in which the author tells of the wider implications of his subject; other scholars might well regard them as invitations awaiting acceptance. In fact I hope Professor Thrower rereads them from time to time himself and, stimulated by them, that he will start preparing for a second expedition.

CLARENCE J. GLACKEN
University of California
Berkeley, California

*Dedicated
to the memory
of my father-in-law
John Gregory Martin, M. D.
of Taxila, Pakistan and
Wadsworth, Ohio
1890-1959*

PREFACE

OVER MOST OF THE LAND surface of the earth, unsystematic methods of dividing areas for settlement have been used. In only a few extensive regions, including the western part of the United States, do basic surveys conform to an over-all plan. The purpose of this study is to examine selected elements of the cultural landscape as developed, in areas that are of similar character but differ in the method used for the subdivision of land. Many relevant topics could be treated, but this study is limited to an examination of administrative, property, and field units and lines of transportation. These serve to fragment areas and are regarded as elements significant to man arising from, or related in greater or lesser degree to, the fundamental division of land for settlement, ownership, and taxation—the cadastral survey.

Two localities in the western half of Ohio have been studied in detail and are used to exemplify different survey systems. For these purposes other areas might have been chosen, but Ohio was selected because, in addition to exhibiting these contrasting types of land subdivision, unusually complete records at all levels are available for that state. It is not the intention in this study to provide an account of methods of land subdivision throughout history, nor to outline the manner in which particular surveys are conducted. These topics, which have been the subject of various treatises, will be touched upon in this work only by way of introduction or to give coherence to particular ideas. Nor will an examination be made of modifications of landscape patterns developed upon different types of land surface subdivided by the same method, although this might well be a fruitful investigation.

A comparison of selected features of the cultural landscape, arising in areas similar in their physical characteristics but subdivided according to different systems of cadastral survey, is attempted in this monograph. Some of the methods of historical geography are employed but this is not intended to be a general historical geography of particular localities. The areas studied are important in this work only insofar as they illuminate the topic, which concerns the form and effect of cadastral surveys. Thus it is a systematic study and an approach to the geography of land subdivision; it deals with a phase of rural geography and, because of its dependence on maps, might be considered cultural cartography. Some of the most important factors will perforce be omitted or slighted. For example, the spatial arrangement of habitations, to name one element of the visible landscape, which may be related to original surveys, will not be discussed in this work, which focuses upon land subdivision of two very dissimilar types and at different periods. However, some elements (e.g., certain boundaries) which may have no visible expression in the landscape will be studied. The examination of land areas and their limits, including those resulting from road construction, in two similar areas subdivided by contrasting methods of cadastral survey is the prime concern of this work. While it is evident that the qualities of a basic cadastral survey system should strongly affect the lineaments of resulting occupance and use of the land, few attempts have been made to describe and measure these effects with any precision. The present study was undertaken in an effort to fill part of this void.

Acknowledgment is due many persons who have contributed to this work. Special thanks for help and advice are extended to the writer's mentors, Professor Arthur H. Robinson and Professor Andrew H. Clark of the Department of Geography of the University of Wisconsin, Madison, and to Professor Marshall Clagett, formerly of the History of Science Department at the University of Wisconsin and now of the Institute for Advanced Study, Princeton University. Professor Vernon Carstensen, formerly of the History Department, University of Wisconsin (now at the University of Washington), contributed helpful suggestions, as did Professor John Randall of the Geography Department, Ohio State University. Judge John Coffin of Columbus, Ohio, kindly arranged interviews with senior administrators and thus provided valued assistance to the writer. Many local, state, and federal officials, particularly in Ohio, both those specifically mentioned in the text and others, cooperated by supplying information. The graphs and the maps, drawn in a style used in cadastral surveys, are the work of the writer or of his students, especially David G. Philips and Hiroko Kowta, except those in Figure 9. The photographs in Figures 36, 37, and 38 were taken during the course of field study.

The University of California, Los Angeles, generously supported the study by research grants for library and field work; the latter was undertaken in the summers of 1955, 1959, and 1961. The writer is grateful that those responsible for the A.A.G. Monograph Series selected this study for publication. It was a particularly pleasant and rewarding experience for the writer to work with the Editor of the Series, Professor Clarence J. Glacken of the Department of Geography, University of California, Berkeley, whose scholarly criticisms greatly enhance the monograph. W. Philip Gerould, Editor, Natural Sciences, College Department, of Rand McNally conferred with the editor and writer in California; this visit and his continued interest in the work are acknowledged with thanks. Finally the writer wishes to express his appreciation to various members of his family and, especially, to his wife Betty for constant help and encouragement.

NORMAN J. W. THROWER

University of California

Los Angeles, California

June 1965

Allen Fehr, 22, died at Mercy Hospital in Fort Dodge early Wednesday morning of injuries suffered in a one-car accident. According to Highway Patrolman, D. W. Homan of Humboldt, who investigated, Fehr en route south had just passed a car and in returning to the right side of the road lost control of his vehicle. The car went into the ditch on the west side of the road. Fehr was thrown from the car. The site of the tragedy is at a point where Humboldt, Kossuth, Palo Alto and Pocahontas counties meet.

Fehr was traveling in Palo Alto county until he passed the car and moved to the other side of the highway which is in Kossuth county. The car went into the ditch in Pocahontas county and Fehr's body was thrown about 100 feet into Humboldt county.

From the *Fort Dodge* (Iowa) *Messenger*
August 4th, 1961

CONTENTS

LIST OF ILLUSTRATIONS

Figures

Tables

Appendices

Figure 1a   Aerial Photograph of an Area in Northwestern Ohio Subdivided in the Manner of the United States Land Survey System. The black crosses indicate a quarter section (½ x ½ mile).

Figure 1b   Aerial Photograph of an Area in the Virginia Military District of Ohio Subdivided in an Unsystematic Manner. Figures 1a and 1b are from the Commodity Stabilization Service (formerly Production and Marketing Administration) of the U. S. Department of Agriculture and are of a uniform scale.

I.

Introduction

INSCRIBED UPON THAT GRAND DESIGN, the surface of the earth, are the marks of human occupance. Patterns resulting from man's activities, although individually not of the great scale of some natural features, in aggregate give to certain areas their most distinctive character. Of all the works of man, one of the most widespread, if not the most important, is the subdivision of land. Once laid down, the boundaries of land divisions become part of man's inheritance to be accepted or modified by later generations.

The complex nature of patterns appearing on the face of the earth is perhaps most evident from above, and it is through air travel that they have become familiar to large numbers of people. Such patterns are strikingly illustrated by air photographs. Figures 1a and 1b are vertical air photographs of two areas which are remarkably alike, apart from differences produced by man. Certain of these man-made features, such as field boundaries and roads, are immediately evident from inspection of the two photographs. In Figure 1a, fields are generally rectangular in shape with boundaries oriented in cardinal directions. Field boundaries in Figure 1b, by contrast, are oriented in any and all directions and enclose patches of land of different shapes. Roads in Figure 1a are also commonly oriented in

cardinal directions and are spaced at specific intervals. In Figure
1b, roads extend over the area in an irregular fashion in all
directions. Field patterns and roads are only two phenomena
which have been selected to illustrate the differences which exist
between the areas shown in Figures 1a and 1b. Maps of these two
areas reveal other differences, the result of man's work, which
are either not discernible in the photographs or require interpretation, for example, property and administrative boundaries.

The reason for many differences in these two areas, similar in
physical character, developed under the same state government
and separated by only a small distance in space, is to be found, in
large measure, in the contrasting methods of land subdivision
used.[1] The land in Figure 1a was surveyed in the systematic,
rectangular manner of the United States National Land System,
while the land in Figure 1b was subdivided unsystematically.
Ohio is a meeting place for different methods of land subdivision (Figure 2); before discussing reasons for this, the general
nature of the two surveys exemplified by Figures 1a and 1b will
be considered.

Under the unsystematic type of survey (Figure 1b), base lines
and markers for individual land holdings are arbitrarily se-

[1]Preston E. James and Clarence F. Jones (Editors), *American Geography, Inventory
and Prospect*, Syracuse, 1954, p. 128. In Chapter 5 of this volume, "Settlement
Geography" by Clyde F. Kohn with the cooperation of Robert E. Dickinson,
Robert B. Hall, and Fred B. Kniffen, it is suggested that although American
geographers have not devoted much attention to the geometry of land occupance, "... there are contrasts in settlement patterns in North America that
would repay careful investigation." This reference came to the writer's notice
after he had already embarked on the present study. Among outstanding studies
related to this topic by American geographers are Carlton P. Barnes, "Economies of the Long Lot Farm," *Geographical Review*, Vol. 25, 1935, pp. 298-301, and
Hildegard Binder Johnson, "Rational and Ecological Aspects of the Quarter
Section," *Geographical Review*, Vol. 47, 1957, pp. 330-348. The first deals particularly with cost and the second with conservational aspects of land subdivision,
two attributes which are not emphasized in this work.

The importance of land subdivision as an element in the visible, cultural
landscape is dramatically shown in "space" photography. Even when other
patterns such as lines of transportation and settlements are poorly represented
or lost in such photos, which are taken at an average of one hundred miles
away from the earth, the cadastral survey systems can be discerned. One excellent example of this of many that might be cited appears in photograph number
14, spool number 1, Gemini V, where the regularity of subdivision in the
Imperial Valley of California, north of the international boundary, contrasts
with the less regular nature of such patterns south of this boundary in Mexico.

lected. These lines and markers are often natural features such as streams and ridges or objects like trees or stones. It is now customary to survey (with instruments) straight lines between markers, but these lines do not conform to an over-all plan. The result of this type of land subdivision is a patchwork of properties, which occasionally overlap each other. In addition, the description of land holdings in an unsystematic survey relies, generally, on features which have only a temporary existence, so that disputes commonly arise from this mode of settlement. Unsystematic surveys are known variously as metes and bounds[2] and indiscriminate location, but the term unsystematic will be used in this study.[3] Most of the world's land areas have been subdivided unsystematically, and this lack of system explains, in part, the complicated pattern of property and civil boundaries in many older settled regions of the earth. The greater part of the area of the original thirteen states of the United States was subdivided unsystematically under local control (Figure 2).[4] The

[2]*McGraw-Hill Encyclopedia of Science and Technology,* New York, 1960, Vol. 13, p. 329, defines this type of land subdivision in these terms: "A metes and bounds survey is a closed traverse around a property. Its description identifies a point of beginning, gives the sequence of distances and directions, identifies the angle points, and notes the fact of return to the point of beginning." Some workers have assumed that a metes and bounds survey implies the use of the magnetic compass and thus that this method is a special case of indiscriminate or unsystematic cadastral survey.

[3]Meredith F. Burrill of the United States Board on Geographic Names indicated in conversation that indiscriminate is an especially inappropriate term for these surveys where the claimants were most discriminating in their choice of locations.

[4]Francis J. Marschner, *Land Use and Its Patterns in the United States, Agricultural Handbook No. 153,* United States Department of Agriculture, Washington, D.C., 1959, p. 20, and by the same author, *Boundaries and Records in the Territory of Early Settlement from Canada to Florida with Historical Notes on the Cadaster and Its Potential Value in the Area,* United States Department of Agriculture, Washington, D.C., 1960, opp. p. 1. Marschner's excellent Map of Land Division Types in the United States is reproduced in both of these works. Mr. Marschner suggested in conversation that air photographs were indispensable to his delimitation of the boundaries of the various survey areas. Included within the area of systematic surveys are several variants, those applying to Ohio being summarized in Appendix A of the present study. The area of unsystematic surveys also exhibits a number of variations, including the riparian long lot. On Marschner's original map different symbols are used for the "New England" type of land subdivision and that used elsewhere in the colonies. Although this distinction is useful for certain purposes, it has not been retained in this study because, although there was a greater uniformity in occupance patterns in localities settled in the township manner in New England, no over-all plan applied to the subdivisions of

same general method applies to the larger part of Kentucky, Tennessee, and eastern Texas, as well as smaller areas of some other states including New Mexico and California. The Virginia Military District of Ohio, from which the small area shown in Figure 1b was taken, is another locality with unsystematic land subdivision.

The rectangular survey of the United States National Land System is a method of land subdivision very different from the unsystematic survey described above. Figure 1a shows a small part of Ohio surveyed under the rectangular system. Except for a few areas, this systematic method of survey was used over all of the western part of the United States (Figure 2). North America is the most extensive area of the world over which uniform systems of land survey extend. Detailed instructions concerning the method of land subdivision to be employed in the western areas of the United States were contained in a land ordinance enacted by Congress on May 20, 1785.[5] This Land Ordinance of 1785 and subsequent land acts have been lauded as outlining a method of surveying which "was an astonishing advance over systems used elsewhere in the world . . ."[6] and as being among "the few important state papers upon which the fundamental rights of mankind are founded."[7] "It proved," said Payson J. Treat, "to be one of the wisest and most influential . . . of all the acts of the Revolutionary Period."[8] The essential features of the National Land System as applied to the remainder of the public domain were worked out in the Old Northwest, as the result of

a considerable area in that region. Hence the New England township was a social phenomenon rather than a system of surveys. Canada, like the United States, has a variety of geometrical cadastral surveys including rectangular (with and without provision for road easements) and the rare "round" type (with radial subdivisions), as well as unsystematic riparian long-lot surveys, etc.

[5] *Journals of the American Congress,* Washington, D.C., 1823, Vol. 4, pp. 520-524. This is the third reading of "An ordinance for ascertaining the mode of disposing of lands in the Western Territory."

[6] C. E. Sherman, *Original Ohio Land Subdivisions,* Vol. 3, Final Report, Ohio Cooperative Topographic Survey, Columbus, 1925, p. 38.

[7] William E. Peters, *Ohio Lands and Their Subdivisions,* Athens, Ohio, 1918, p. 52. Sherman praises Peters' legal contribution to improved understanding of land problems in Ohio. Sherman, *op. cit.,* p. 7.

[8] Payson J. Treat, *The National Land System 1785-1820,* New York, 1910, p. 40.

experience of land subdivision in that area.[9] Elements which are of particular concern in this study are (1) survey prior to settlement, (2) orientation of survey lines, (3) the township unit, and (4) the section.

Although well known, it is perhaps desirable here to recall briefly the main characteristics of the United States National Land System. In the rectangular survey of the United States, two fundamental lines govern an original survey tract — one, N-S, called a principal meridian and the other, E-W, designated a principal base or parallel. These lines meet or cross at right angles at some point in advance of land already subdivided.[10] Lines (called range lines) are surveyed at intervals of 6 miles parallel to the principal meridian and are numbered E and W of this line.

The principal parallel is a beginning place for township lines, spaced at intervals of 6 miles, and numbered N and S of this principal base. The resulting areas of approximately 6 x 6 miles enclosed by the two systems of parallel lines are known as townships; all are not perfect squares owing to the convergence of meridians and to errors in surveying. To overcome these difficulties, correction lines are established at prescribed intervals from principal bases and from the principal meridians.[11] Each township is subdivided into 36 one-square-mile plots known as sections; these are numbered 1 to 36.[12] By this system any parcel of land can be located by reference to its section, township, and range numbers within the particular original survey tract. Thus the ½ mile-square area enclosed by black crosses on Figure 1a is the N.W. quarter, Section 15 Township

[9]Frank M. Johnson, *The Rectangular System of Surveying,* Department of the Interior, General Land Office, Washington, D.C., 1924.

[10]Fundamentally, it is to this initial point—the intersection of a principal meridian and a base line—that the surveys in a particular area in the United States Public Land System are referred.

[11]Correction lines in the early surveys appear irregularly, but later, and ideally, every 24-square-mile tract is bounded by standard parallels on the north and south and by guide meridians on the east and west.

[12]See the map in Appendix B of this work for various methods of numbering sections. Type Z of that illustration, as employed in Northwestern Ohio, was the numbering system adopted for subsequent United States Public Land Surveys.

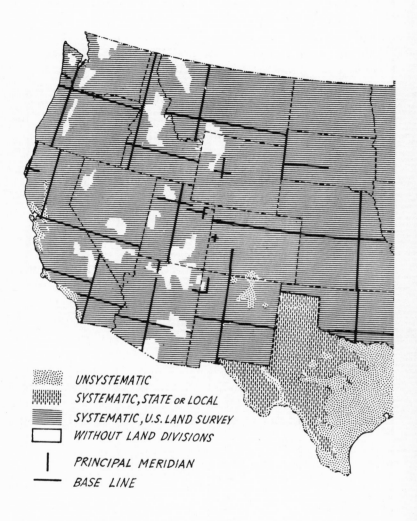

Figure 2 Land Subdivision Types in the Coterminous United States. (Adapted and simplified from Francis J. Marschner, *Land Use and Its Patterns in the United States, Agricultural Handbook No. 153*. United States

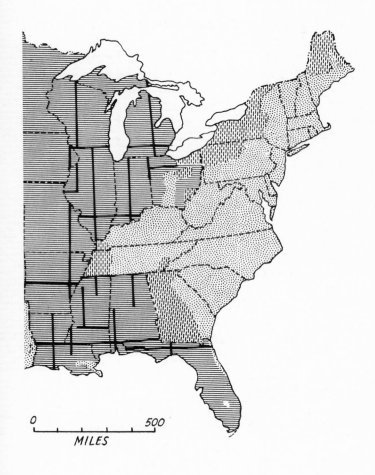

Department of Agriculture, Washington, D.C., 1959, p. 20, and C. E. Sherman, *Ohio Land Subdivisions,* Vol. III, Final Report, Ohio Cooperative Topographic Survey, Columbus, 1925, frontispiece.)

2 South, Range 10 East of the First Principal Meridian (S 15, T 2 S, R 10 E, 1st PM). In the United States there are 34 principal meridians governing the same number of original survey areas, which range in size from a few hundred to several thousand square miles (Figure 2).

SYSTEMATIC LAND SUBDIVISION BEFORE 1785

The broad features of the Land Ordinance of 1785 were contained in a report presented to Congress in the previous year.[13] This report was prepared by a committee under the chairmanship of Thomas Jefferson, but it must not be supposed that a piece of legislation so broadly conceived was exclusively the brainchild of this committee and was without precedent in the experience of those framing the Ordinance. Amelia Clewley Ford, in a dissertation written under the historian Frederick Jackson Turner, indicates that the men in Congress drew heavily upon their knowledge of colonial land policies.[14] Dr. Ford shows, in her study, that a continuity exists between colonial land systems and the system framed by the national legislators between 1785 and 1800. A prominent authority on Ohio surveys, C. E. Sherman, attempted to sketch the origin of systematic surveys before the American colonial period.[15]

Aerial photographs and excavations have revealed the existence of gridiron patterns in early town plans in the Indus Valley.[16] The Romans divided lands, to be colonized and distributed to

---

[13]*Journals of the American Congress,* Vol. 4, Government Printing Office, Washington, D.C., 1923, entry under March 1, 1784, pp. 342-343. This matter has recently been the subject of a detailed study by William D. Pattison in his doctoral dissertation, *Beginnings of the American Rectangular Land Survey System, 1784-1800,* Department of Geography, Research Paper No. 50, University of Chicago, Chicago, 1957, and by the same author, "The Original Plan for an American Rectangular Land Survey," *Surveying and Mapping,* Vol. 21, No. 3, September, 1961, pp. 339-345.

[14]Amelia Clewley Ford, *Colonial Precedents of Our National Land System As It Existed in 1800: Bulletin of the University of Wisconsin No. 352,* Madison, 1910, pp. 321-477.

[15]Sherman, *op. cit.,* pp. 215-225.

[16]Sir John H. Marshall, *Mohenjo-Daro and the Indus Valley Civilization,* London, 1931, plates 1 and 2, and also later photographs taken in 1958 of Charsada, near Peshawar, by the Pakistan Air Force at the request of Sir Mortimer Wheeler, who was then directing excavations nearby.

veterans, into rectangular sections; evidence of this can still be seen in the landscape of Italy and other parts of the Roman Empire.[17] To facilitate systematic land subdivision before the advent of the magnetic compass in Europe, the Romans used a *groma*, a surveying instrument with four arms set at 90° to each other, with which they established the corners of the rectangular plots. A *groma* was found among the ruins at Pompeii.[18] Systematic methods of land subdivision were also employed on the polders of Holland during the seventeenth century.[19] In his capacity as Surveyor General of Ireland (1655-1656), under the Protectorate, the political economist, Sir William Petty, initiated geometrical surveys of military-warrant lands.[20] Ideas of land subdivision from these and other sources apparently were available to the American colonists.

The charters of some of the colonies specified regular outlines to the north and south, where parallels were used as boundaries. Sometimes meridians served as the western boundaries of colonies as, for example, in the case of Pennsylvania.[21] A rectangular ground plan was employed for several important colonial cities: New Haven, Philadelphia, Charleston, and Savannah were laid out in this fashion. Outside of the cities the land was, at first, subdivided irregularly. In New England there was less irregularity than elsewhere in rural areas because of the township system.[22] Under this type of colonization, civil town-

[17]John Bradford, *Ancient Landscapes*, London, 1957. In Chapter 4 (pp. 145-216) of this work, Roman centuriation is discussed and the literature on the subject examined. Air photos of planned landscapes from France to Dalmatia and from North Italy to Tunisia, showing present effects of Roman centuriation, illustrate the chapter. See also George Kish, "Centuriatio: The Roman Rectangular Land Survey," *Surveying and Mapping*, Vol. 22, No. 2, June, 1962, pp. 233-244.
[18]Don Gelasio Caetani, "The 'Groma' or Cross Bar of the Roman Surveyor," *Engineering and Mining Journal-Press*, November 29, 1924, p. 855.
[19]Sherman, *op. cit.*, pp. 221-222.
[20]John P. Prendergast, *The Cromwellian Settlement of Ireland*, 2nd ed., Dublin, 1875, pp. 187-244 and maps. In addition, see Thomas A. Larcom (Editor), *The History of the Down Survey by Doctor William Petty*, Dublin, 1851, p. 3.
[21]Thomas Donaldson, *The Public Domain*, Government Printing Office, Washington, D.C., 1884, p. 46. In this work, various colonial charters are reviewed with significant portions of the originals extracted and rendered in modern language.
[22]Melville Egleston, *The Land System of the New England Colonies*, Johns Hopkins Studies in Historical and Political Science, Fourth Series, 11-12, Baltimore, 1886. Also see Marschner, *Boundaries and Records, op. cit.*, pp. 215-219.

ships of fairly equal size were laid out, usually along a route or river. These units were rarely square or consistently oriented over a large area but they were frequently bounded by straight lines. They were often subdivided prior to settlement and contained multiple lots, but the internal units of the township were, characteristically, not of uniform size or shape.

Idealistic schemes for the systematic subdivision of land in some of the southern colonies were proposed. John Locke, the philosopher, who apparently was familiar with Petty's survey of Ireland, concerned himself with matters affecting colonial settlement for his patron, the first Earl of Shaftesbury. Locke developed a plan in 1699, known as the Grand Model, whereby the colony of South Carolina was to be divided into squares of 12,000 acres (townships), which were to be combined into counties.[23] In 1717, Sir Robert Montgomery, a proprietor of part of the area now Georgia, drew up a plan for the systematic subdivision of his lands into square districts, to be divided into smaller squares.[24] These two proposals for the settlement of land in the rural South, although not seriously developed, reveal that for parts of that region systematic surveys were under consideration. A most comprehensive plan for the regular subdivision of land in colonial times was devised by Colonel Henry Bouquet, an officer fighting the Ohio Indians on the western frontier. Bouquet's conception was of townships organized and settled as a defense against Indian attacks; his scheme anticipates the system adopted by the national legislators in a number of ways. It is noteworthy that Bouquet, who was Swiss by birth, in the course of his travels visited several parts of Europe where he could have observed the effects of systematic land surveys.[25] Thomas Hutchins, who later became the Geographer of the United States, or

[23]W. D. Christie, *A Life of Anthony Ashley Cooper, First Earl of Shaftesbury,* London, 1871, Vol. 1, pp. 288-289, and Ford, *op. cit.,* pp. 329-332.

[24]Charles C. Jones, Jr., *The History of Georgia,* Boston, 1883, Vol. I, pp. 70-75 and map opposite p. 72.

[25]William Smith (Dr.), *Historical Account of Bouquet's Expedition Against the Ohio Indians in 1764,* Cincinnati, Ohio, 1868, pp. xvii-xxiii. Also pp. 119-122, illustration p. 121. Bouquet's proposal involved squares of 640 acres each, arranged in contiguous townships. Thomas Hutchins, who drew the maps for the *Historical Account of Bouquet's Expedition,* is sometimes credited with the authorship of this work. See p. xv.

first officer in charge of government surveys in Ohio, served under Bouquet on the frontier prior to 1764.

The report presented by Jefferson's committee to Congress in 1784 set forth a proposal for a rectangular system of surveys to be used in the public domain. Recently, William D. Pattison has stressed the special importance of the contribution of one of the committee members, Hugh Williamson of North Carolina, to the United States Land Survey System.[26] Before being approved by Congress, the plan was altered in several particulars, which are discussed at length by Pattison. The system that was finally adopted and passed into law as the Land Ordinance of 1785 applied only to the area of Ohio now known as the Seven Ranges. However, this provided the fundamental model or pattern which was modified as surveys progressed in the Ohio country.

TERRITORIAL CLAIMS OF THE COLONIES

In an earlier section of this chapter some results of two contrasting survey systems used in Ohio have been illustrated. To understand the reasons for the employment, in this area, of these different methods of land subdivision, it is necessary to consider briefly some of the events which led up to the opening of the Old Northwest for permanent white settlement.

Title to western lands, a problem in the colonial period, became a pressing matter at the time of the Declaration of Independence. Six of the former colonies, Massachusetts, Connecticut, Virginia, North Carolina, South Carolina, and Georgia, had claims to unexplored or unsettled lands to the west based on their ancient charters.[27] New York as suzerain of the Iroquois Indians had title to a large area west of the Delaware River. A number of these claims overlapped (Figure 3). The remaining six states had definite boundaries and could claim no lands west of the Alleghenies. Among the states without western lands, Maryland was a leader in opposing the idea of state title to land

---

[26]Pattison, *Beginnings of the American Rectangular Land Survey System, 1784-1800,* pp. 38 and 226.
[27]Donaldson, *op. cit.,* pp. 30-55.

in the West and refused to ratify the Articles of Confederation until the question was resolved.[28] In 1778 a committee of Congress proposed that cessions of western lands be made by the claimant states; the following year Virginia and other states were urged to cease granting western lands during the war.[29] An important step toward the settlement of the problem was made

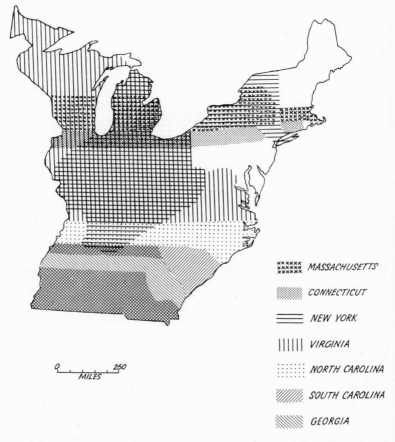

0 ——— 250
MILES

MASSACHUSETTS

CONNECTICUT

NEW YORK

VIRGINIA

NORTH CAROLINA

SOUTH CAROLINA

GEORGIA

Figure 3 Land Claims of Colonies (Later States of the United States). (Adapted from Maps B, C, D, and E of Plate 47 from Charles O. Paullin, *Atlas of the Historical Geography of the United States,* John K. Wright (Editor), Washington, D.C., 1932.)

[28]*Journals of Congress, op. cit.,* Vol. 2, p. 598.
[29]*Ibid.,* Vol. 3, p. 383.

Figure 4 The Public Domain of the United States Prior to the Louisiana Purchase, 1803. (Adapted from the map, "United States, Showing the Extent of Public Surveys," 1953, U. S. Department of the Interior, Bureau of Land Management, and Plates 46C and 47D, Paullin, *op. cit.*)

when New York, in February 1780, defined her own limits and ceded lands beyond these boundaries to the United States.[30]

At the conclusion of the Revolutionary War, the western land question was again before the legislators of the republic. All states had contributed lives, goods, and treasure to the United States; all felt that they had a claim to the financial if not the political advantages of ownership of western lands. The matter was solved when other states, following the lead of New York, ceded their claims to western lands to the United States. This was done only after considerable discussion and with reservations on the part of some of the affected states.[31] By 1784 the United States assumed control of a vast area in the West (Figure 4). This national or public domain did not extend from sea to sea as claimed by the colonial charters, which were based on the old assumption of a continent of very limited longitudinal extent. The Mississippi River, which was controlled by the French, provided a western limit to the ceded area. Even so, the public lands acquired before the Louisiana Purchase in 1803 amounted to over 400,000 square miles,[32] an area larger than the total territory which remained under the immediate control of the thirteen original states after their cessions of western land.

[30]*Ibid.*, Vol. 3, pp. 582-586.
[31]*Loc. cit.*, p. 582.
[32]Donaldson, *op. cit.*, p. 88.

II.

Survey Districts and Example Areas

REFERENCE HAS BEEN MADE to two contrasting types of land subdivision — the rectangular and the unsystematic. It was the intention of the federal government to use one method of survey for the public domain when the Land Ordinance was passed by Congress in 1785.[1] Actually, systematic, rectangular survey in Ohio varies from one major survey area to another in matters such as the size and numbering of townships, and of their internal divisions (sections). The state has been described as "the experimental station" for the evolving National Land System.[2] In this chapter we are directly concerned only with example areas and the two larger survey tracts from which they are derived — the Virginia Military District and Northwestern Ohio. However, in Appendices A and B an attempt has been made to classify in tabular and graphical form the major methods of land subdivision used in Ohio.

[1]*Journals of the American Congress,* Washington, D.C., 1823, Vol. 4, p. 520.
[2]William E. Peters, *Ohio Lands and Their Subdivisions,* Athens, Ohio, 1918, p. 69. Part of southern Indiana which was surveyed before Northwestern Ohio shared in this "evolution," Frank M. Johnson, *The Rectangular System of Surveying,* Department of the Interior, General Land Office, Washington, D.C., 1924.

THE VIRGINIA MILITARY DISTRICT OF OHIO

It has been indicated that the cessions of some states were accompanied by reservations. Only the reservation of Virginia affecting an area now in Ohio (i.e., the Virginia Military District), however, need be dealt with here. Virginia's title to western lands rested on an earlier charter than those of the other states, and her claim was more extensive (Figure 3). All of the area now Ohio was claimed by both Virginia and New York; the northern third was demanded by Connecticut as well as by the other two states. It was Virginia's second charter, granted to the London Company by King James I in May, 1609, that extended the territorial limits of the colony

> . . . from the point of land, called Cape or Point Comfort, all along the sea coast, to the northward two hundred miles, and from the said point of Cape Comfort, all along the sea coast to the southward two hundred miles; and all that space and circuit of land, lying from the sea coast of the precinct aforesaid, up into the land, throughout from sea to sea, west and northwest . . .[3]

The request by the United States for cessions of western land at length met with a favorable response from Virginia. That state authorized her delegates in Congress in September, 1783,[4] to convey to the federal government, subject to a condition, her rights to the land in the territory northwest of the Ohio River — rights over soil as well as jurisdiction. The condition was that if she did not have sufficient land in Kentucky to meet bounty claims which she authorized to troops of the Virginia Revolutionary Establishment, the state might make up such a deficiency in good land between the Scioto and Little Miami rivers. Virginia war-bounty warrants were particularly generous, and a deficiency of lands southeast of the Ohio River was reported in

[3]William W. Hening, *The Statutes at Large: Being a Collection of All of the Laws of Virginia,* Vol. 1, New York, 1823, p. 88. This appears to be the earliest use of the term "northwest" as it was applied, successively, to various frontier areas from Ohio to Oregon.
[4]*Journals of Congress, op. cit.,* Vol. 4, pp. 265-267.

1790.[5] In that year the first officially approved surveys of land to satisfy bounty claims were begun in the Virginia Military District of Ohio.

The District is not bounded entirely by the Scioto and Little Miami rivers, for in the northwest of the area the headwaters of the two streams are separated by approximately fifty miles. When surveys were begun to the west of the Virginia Military District, it became necessary to define boundaries precisely. The Greenville Treaty Line, separating Indian lands to the north from lands available for white settlement to the south, was laid off in 1797.[6] This line cuts across the northern portion of the Virginia Military District (Figure 5). A government surveyor, Israel Ludlow, ran a line from the source of the Little Miami to the Greenville Treaty Line at about N 15° W. Ludlow's line, subject to approval of the State of Virginia, was adopted by Congress as the western boundary of the District. Virginia objected, and a new line was run by Charles Roberts from the source of the Little Miami River at about N 20° W; at a point 11.5 miles north of the Greenville Treaty Line, Roberts' line turned almost at right angles to meet the supposed source of the Scioto, two miles to the east (Figure 5). At first, the representatives of Virginia would accept neither Ludlow's nor Roberts' line, but after much discussion the boundary of the Virginia Military District was confirmed as follows: the Little Miami River from mouth to source, Ludlow's line to the Greenville Treaty Line, westward on this line to Roberts' line, Roberts' line to the source of the Scioto, the Scioto from source to mouth and the Ohio River from the mouth of the Scioto to the mouth of the Little Miami.[7]

---

[5]Samuel M Wilson, *Catalogue of Revolutionary Soldiers and Sailors of the Commonwealth of Virginia, (Virginia Revolutionary Land Bounty Warrants)*, Baltimore, 1953, p. 2. This work lists the names of the earlier warrant holders; the rank of the claimant, his warrant number, date of the warrant, size of the claim and other pertinent information is recorded, e.g., "685, Smith, Obadiah, 2666 2/3 acres, Lieutenant, Va. Cont. Line, 3 yrs, May 30, 1783" (p. 66). See entry following footnote 28 of the present chapter.
[6]Peters, *op. cit.*, p. 99. By some authorities (e.g., Treat), this important survey line and the treaty after which it is named are spelled Greeneville.
[7]C. E. Sherman, *Original Ohio Land Subdivisions*, Vol. 3, Final Report, Ohio Cooperative Topographic Survey, Columbus 1925, pp. 27-28.

Legal surveys to fulfill the Virginia military-bounty warrants began in Ohio in 1790. The warrants were for parcels of land from 100 to 15,000 acres; each bore a different number.[8] There was no restriction as to the shape of a plot, and all of any particular warrant was not required to be in one contiguous parcel of land. Although the earliest surveys were generally made in the southern part of the Virginia Military District, this was by no means always the case. A warrant holder (or more often his agent or assignee) would go into the area and lay off the best piece or pieces of land he could secure. This usually meant plots bordering a river at first. In many instances, warrant holders enclosed more land than they were entitled to; Sherman cites one example of a warrant which called for 450 acres, although actually over 1,500 acres were enclosed.[9] There were overlapping claims and, conversely, some areas were not claimed at all.[10] Many warrant holders did not occupy, or even visit, their own lands in the Virginia Military District but rather sold them through agents in Eastern cities. Although the military warrants were the basic units for the transfer of land, most were soon divided into properties. In 1871 all lands not claimed in the Virginia Military District were ceded by the federal government to the State of Ohio.[11]

NORTHWESTERN OHIO

This was the last major part of Ohio to be settled, and the plan of survey employed here was used for all subsequent subdivisions of the public domain of the United States. The survey began in

[8]Wilson, *op. cit.* These warrant numbers are not the same as the Virginia Military District unit numbers which were assigned by the Surveyor General of the Land Office in Virginia. It was from this office that a qualified Virginia Revolutionary War Veteran secured a printed warrant specifying the quantity of land he was due. The warrant empowered the grantee or his heirs or assignees to select the number of acres specified and to have the area surveyed. After this was accomplished, a patent was issued which was the equivalent of a deed in fee simple, passing title from the government to the grantee. Theoretically, a grant as large as 17,500 acres was possible.

[9]Sherman, *op. cit.*, p. 32.

[10]Survey No. 12566 of the Virginia Military District illustrates this last point; see Peters, *op. cit.*, pp. 23-24 and the accompanying map.

[11]Thomas Donaldson, *The Public Domain*, Government Printing Office, Washington, D.C., 1884, pp. 233-234.

the area in 1819, after a series of treaties with the Indians had prepared the way for white settlement.[12] The last Indian reservation in the region was not ceded to the national government until 1842. With the exception of a few small areas, Northwestern

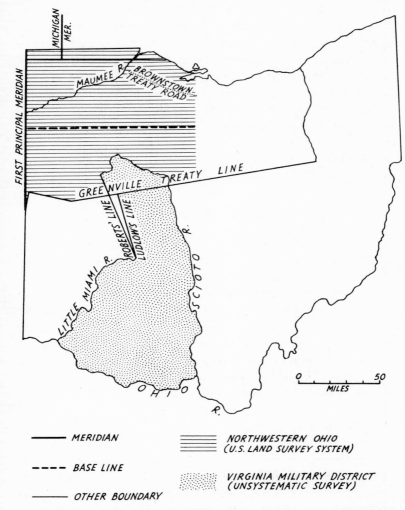

Figure 5 Selected Fundamental Survey Lines and Areas in Ohio (after Sherman, *op. cit.*, and others). For details of other major survey areas in Ohio see Appendices A and B.

[12]Payson J. Treat, *The National Land System 1785-1820*, New York, 1910, especially Chapter 7, pp. 162-178, map p. 164.

Ohio is uniformly subdivided; areas that do not conform to the rectangular plan include a narrow strip along the Brownstown Treaty Road and some old settlements near the mouth of the Maumee River. The strip of land bordering the Michigan boundary, the most northerly part of the survey district (Figure 5), is subdivided in the manner of the National Land System but is governed by different meridians and base lines than those of the remainder of Northwestern Ohio. With the exceptions noted above, ranges in Northwestern Ohio are numbered east from the Ohio-Indiana line (the First Principal Meridian of the United States Land Survey), and townships are numbered *regularly* N and S of a base line. This base is parallel to, and a few seconds south of latitude 41° N. Over most of its area, Northwestern Ohio is representative of the original surveys of the United States Public Land System.

GENERAL AREA

To make feasible the examination of certain detailed characteristics in this work, it was decided to study small example areas. This method was employed to prevent the work from becoming unnecessarily protracted, to eliminate some apparently unrepresentative areas, and to make possible the use of the air photograph as a research tool. Furthermore, it was felt, after experimental work was undertaken with other samples, that little of significance would be added to the question at hand by studying larger areas. To make the most valid comparison, it was desirable to find areas that are generally similar, except in the method by which the land was originally subdivided. As a result of careful examination, two example areas were chosen, one from the rectangularly surveyed area of Northwestern Ohio, and one from the unsystematically surveyed Virginia Military District.

In the selection of the two example areas, many factors were taken into account, but it was decided that the landscape characteristics most pertinent to this study included the following: (a) land forms, (b) local relief, (c) lithology, (d) soils, (e) climate, (f) agriculture, and (g) population. The above are not necessarily listed in order of importance. Studies and maps covering these

and other characteristics for Ohio were consulted. The map,
Figure 6, resulted from these investigations; the unshaded portion of the map is regarded as a relatively homogeneous area
except with regard to the manner in which it was surveyed.

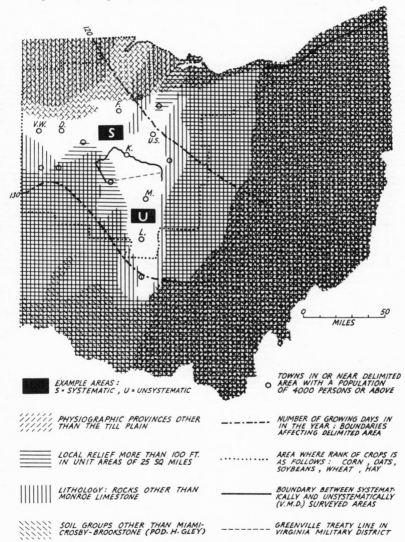

Figure 6 Selected Physical and Cultural Phenomena in Ohio (compiled
from various sources as indicated in the text).

Amplification of points (a) to (g) above, details of sources used, and the method employed to construct the map follow.

(a) Land Forms

Three major physiographic provinces are generally recognized in Ohio: the Appalachian Plateau, the Lake Plain, and the Till Plain. The Appalachian Plateau covers most of the eastern part of the state and consists of quite dissected country. The Lake Plain, an extremely level area, much of which is artificially drained, extends along the Lake Erie shore in a narrow ribbon and widens to cover a large part of Northwestern Ohio. These two physiographic provinces are both indicated by the same broken diagonal shading (sinister) but are separated by a fine line in the upper right-hand corner of Figure 6 where they are in juxtaposition. The third physiographic province, the Till Plain, occupies much of western Ohio and differs from the Lake Plain in being better drained and having a more undulating, but still subdued surface. The Till Plain is not shaded with the diagonal lines used for the other physiographic provinces. Lines separating these provinces were taken from the map of Physical Divisions of the United States by Nevin Fenneman.[13]

(b) Local Relief

The horizontal shading on Figure 6 indicates areas in Ohio with a local relief of more than 100 feet in units of approximately 25 square miles; the unshaded areas have a local relief of less than 100 feet in similar units. The information is adapted from Guy-Harold Smith's map of the relative relief of Ohio.[14] Several local relief categories are shown on Professor Smith's map, but the only large section of Ohio in the lowest relief category (0-100

---

[13]Nevin M. Fenneman, *Physiography of the Eastern United States,* New York, 1938, Plate II.

[14]Guy-Harold Smith, "The Relative Relief of Ohio," *Geographical Review,* 1935, Vol. 25, p. 277. Professor Smith kindly showed the writer his unpublished slope maps of Ohio, which further emphasize the plains-like nature of this part of the state.

feet) is the northwestern and west central part of the state as delimited on the map.

(c) Lithology

Attention will now be directed particularly to that part of Ohio in the gently rolling Till Plain which has less than 100 feet of local relief according to Professor Smith's definition. Most of this part of Ohio is underlain by Monroe limestone of Silurian/Devonian Age. Vertical lines on Figure 6 indicate rock types other than the Monroe limestone. Much of the vertically shaded area, especially in the western part of Ohio, is predominantly calcareous but with a greater admixture of shale and of different age than the Monroe. Information on the bedrock of Ohio is taken from the geological maps of the state.[15]

(d) Soils

Upon the Monroe and surrounding formations, fertile gray-brown podsolic and humic gley soils are developed. Except in the south, the distribution of this soil association is roughly coincident with the Till Plain physiographic province. Soil associations other than gray-brown podsolic and humic gley are shaded with the broken diagonal lines (dexter). The soils in the unshaded area are likely to exhibit more variety locally according to site than from district to district within the soil region considered broadly.[16] There is little accelerated soil erosion within the unshaded area.[17]

(e) Climate

The climate of the unshaded area on Figure 6 is all Daf (humid continental with a warm summer), according to Trewartha's

---

[15]*Geologic Map of Ohio,* Geological Survey of Ohio, reprinted with revision, 1947.
[16]United States Department of Agriculture, *Soil Associations of the United States,* 1935, map, and *Major Soils of the North-Central Region,* Publication No. 76, compiled by Soil Surveys of States of the North-Central Region of the United States, 1957.
[17]United States Department of Agriculture, *Erosion Survey Map of Ohio,* 1935.

modification of the Köppen system.[18] In Ohio as a whole, three climatic types are distinguished in this system. According to Thornthwaite's classification of the climates of North America (1931), two climatic types are recognized in Ohio.[19] All of the unshaded area on Figure 6 is classified by Thornthwaite as microthermal climate, with an adequate rainfall in all seasons, designated by the symbols BC'r. Detailed maps of the various climatic elements, precipitation, temperature, etc., were examined but no substantial differences were noted in the area left blank except perhaps in the length of the growing season. This characteristic is shown by a dotted and dashed line on Figure 6. Approximately ten more growing days are available in the south as compared with the north of the unshaded area.[20] This unshaded area extends over only about 2° of latitude.

(f) Agriculture

Western Ohio is an important farming area shown on certain maps of agricultural regions as being toward the eastern edge of the Corn Belt. Feed crops and livestock are the leading agricultural products of the region. A useful indicator of the character of agriculture in areas is the combination of crops by rank. John C. Weaver has produced maps of crop combinations, and information from these has been added to Figure 6. The area enclosed by the dotted line on this map delimits the only part of Ohio where the rank of crops is as follows: corn, oats, soybeans, wheat, and hay (descending order).[21] Over much of Ohio corn and oats are the ranking crops, but only in the area enclosed by the dotted line are soybeans also important according to the classification used.

[18]Glenn T. Trewartha, *An Introduction to Climate,* 3rd edition, New York, 1954, Plate 1.
[19]C. Warren Thornthwaite, "The Climates of North America According to a New Classification," *Geographical Review,* 1931, Vol. 21, pp. 633-655.
[20]*Atlas of American Agriculture,* Part II, Section I, "Frost and the Growing Season," United States Department of Agriculture, Washington, D.C., 1920, p. 40.
[21]John C. Weaver, "Crop-Combination Regions in the Middle West," *Geographical Review,* 1954, Vol. 44, pp. 175-200. In this study, crop percentages are related to the total harvested cropland of a particular unit.

(g) *Population*

The part of Ohio left unshaded on the map (Figure 6) has a number of towns of modest size. Findlay (F on the map), 30,344, is the largest city clearly in the unshaded area; other considerable cities are Van Wert (VW) 11,323, Kenton (K) 8,747, Delphos (D) 6,961, London (L) 6,379, Marysville (M) 4,952, and Upper Sandusky (US) 4,941.[22] None of the large urban centers of Ohio is contained in the area. In the unshaded portion of the map (Figure 6), rural population density is fairly even; more detailed information of this characteristic for the example areas is provided subsequently.

The blank area on the map possesses considerable homogeneity in the characteristics outlined above, as in others studied but not discussed (e.g., native vegetation). However, about half of the unshaded area of Figure 6 was subdivided by the systematic rectangular method, and about half by the unsystematic, metes and bounds survey. The heavy continuous line running through Kenton (K) separates these two survey areas. The unshaded portion north of this line is entirely in the rectangular survey area of Northwestern Ohio, which conforms in all respects to the system used for the national survey as applied to the rest of the public domain west to the Pacific Ocean. South of the heavy line is the unsystematic, metes and bounds survey of the Virginia Military District. Here, then, is an area developed under a single state government which is remarkably similar in all characteristics examined except the subdivision of land. From this area, admirably suited for this purpose of studying the effects of survey upon the land, the small example areas were chosen.

EXAMPLE AREAS

After the area of choice for the examples was narrowed by the means indicated above, other factors were considered in making

[22]United States *Census of Population,* "PC (1)-37B, Ohio, 1960," Washington, D.C., 1961.

the final selection and delimitation. It seemed desirable that the example areas should be as close together, geographically, as possible. In the case of the metes and bounds example, it was deemed advisable to take the example area from counties entirely contained within the Virginia Military District. Examination revealed that in the case of counties partly in the Virginia Military District and partly in the area of rectangular survey, some systematic, rectangular characteristics prevail, even in the Virginia Military District portions of the county.

Preliminary study of examples drawn from both the rectangular and the metes and bounds areas suggests that urban places introduce such a multiplicity of complicating factors that the effects of survey alone become more difficult to measure; for example, in some newer suburban developments there has been a conscious attempt to disrupt the uniformity of the rectangular pattern of roads for aesthetic reasons. Therefore, it was decided to take both samples in rural areas — away from the influence of cities. The circles in and around the unshaded portion of Figure 6 mark the centers of towns each with a population in excess of 4,000 persons. The locality north of Kenton (K) on Figure 6 appeared to be a suitable area for the rectangular example; the specific location of this example area was determined by other factors to be considered later. Two areas in the Virginia Military District — one north of Marysville (M), the other south of it — appear to qualify as regions from which the metes and bounds example might be drawn. The area north of Marysville was not selected because it was considered very unrepresentative of the metes and bounds area as a whole. In this region, around the Greenville Treaty Line (dashed line on Figure 6), some attempt was made to subdivide the land systematically, with the Treaty Line being used, in part, as a base. This was the major reason why the area south of Marysville was chosen as the region from which the metes and bounds example was drawn.

The location of the two example areas, S in the rectangular and U in the unsystematic survey, appears in Figure 6. These areas, which will hereafter be referred to simply as S and U, are 100 square miles each (12 x 8.333 . . . miles). The reason for the rectangular shape was merely to allow a convenient side-by-side comparison of the illustrations in the monograph at the largest possible scale.

Interesting and useful comparisons can be made respecting phenomena along civil boundaries. Accordingly, the example areas were chosen so that a considerable as well as a comparable mileage of contemporary county and township lines were included in both examples (Figure 7). In both cases almost all of the example falls in two counties, with one of these counties containing a larger, and the other a smaller share of the example area. Both example areas contain at least one whole civil township (Figure 7, small dashed lines).

With the two example areas tentatively selected, a detailed examination was made of certain characteristics in these locations. The two 100-square-mile areas have approximately the same local relief. In the example area from the rectangular survey, S, there is a difference of 130 feet between the highest and lowest points. There is a difference of 140 feet between the highest and lowest points in the example area from the unsystematic survey, U. Both areas are on a terrain of fairly smooth topography, but there is more "roll" to the land in example S because the Fort Wayne moraine extends across the area. Example U, which is on the Darby Plains, has somewhat gentler slopes than example S generally. However, these terrain differences are of minor importance. The incised valleys of streams, up to 40 feet in extreme cases but usually much less, are perhaps the most dominant land form features.[23]

More significant to the problem at hand was the matter of the density of population in the example areas. In the census reports, rural population is given for minor civil divisions; because, however, the example areas have parts of civil townships within them, one must estimate the number of persons resident

---

[23]Topographic maps of the United States Geological Survey were used in the determination of these morphological characteristics. Parts of four sheets of the scale of 1:62,250 are required to cover the two example areas, as follows: S, Arlington and Bluffton; U, Mechanicsburg and Milford Center Quadrangles. When shown on these topographic maps, the limits of the example areas used in this study, Mr. Charles D. Lee, an abstractor of titles with a long acquaintance with land matters in this part of Ohio, expressed the opinion that they well exemplified, respectively, the two types of cadastral survey examined in this study.

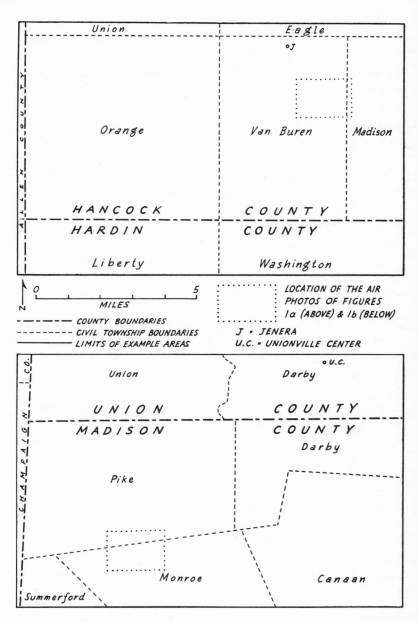

Figures 7a and 7b Map of Example Areas S (above) and U (below) Showing Contemporary Civil Division Boundaries and Other General Information. All maps in this work which follow (except Figures 9a and 9b and the appendix maps) have this format, cover the same areas shown here, and have the same scale and orientation. Figure a is above, Figure b below in the layout, in each case, and legend items are common unless indicated otherwise.

for these parts. Of course there is no problem for townships contained entirely within the example areas; but for those with only a portion of the area in the example an assessment was made. This was accomplished by taking the percentage of the area of the minor civil division contained in the example and ascertaining what this percentage of the total population should be after subtracting the population of all the incorporated places in the entire civil township. If an incorporated place from a civil township only partially contained in an example area fell within the example area, as it did in one case (Unionville Center in U), then it was added to the total (Appendix C). By this means it was estimated that example S and example U each had a population exceeding 2,500 but below 3,000 in 1950 and also in 1960; there was little change in population between the two dates. The only incorporated places in the example areas were Jenera (population 316) in Van Buren Township, which is one of the whole civil townships contained in the example area of rectangular survey, and Unionville Center (population 237), which has been discussed previously as being in one of the civil townships partly in the metes and bounds example area (Figure 7). These two hamlets each occupy only a fraction of one percent of the total land in their respective example areas.[24] The matter of the comparability of the total number of people in the two example areas is especially important in this study, which is concerned with the effects of man's activity.

Man takes with him his culture traits, including methods of using land, when he settles in new areas. In an attempt to measure the effect of this elusive characteristic of cultural inheritance, an effort was made to ascertain the place of birth of the early settlers in areas U and S. Appendix D gives the nativity of persons in the largest whole township in each of the example areas from the 1850 census, the first census to carry this information.[25] By this date both areas had been settled, at least in part,

[24]Jenera and Unionville Center are treated as units for purposes of this study. These hamlets are small service centers in areas in which dispersed rural settlement predominates.

[25]*The Seventh Census of the United States, 1850,* Washington, D.C., 1853. Examination of earlier lists of the first settlers, contained in county histories, atlases, etc., suggests that both in S and U the pioneers were mainly Americans, from both Northern and Southern states. Although there was a predominance of settlers

for several decades, and the inhabitants were predominantly natives of Ohio; no firm conclusions can be drawn from this information. In 1850 there were only a few settlers of foreign birth in either area. Pennsylvanians formed a considerable element of the population in the S townships, which were settled somewhat later than the U townships. There was no strong predominance of persons from any one out-of-state area in U in 1850. Both U and S townships were alike at this time, in that most of the settlers were native Ohioans and that the majority of the persons born outside of Ohio came from the Middle Atlantic states.

No two areas on earth are, of course, exactly alike or have the same physical form, but in all the characteristics examined, the example areas are remarkably similar, except in the matter of the basic subdivision of land. Before proceeding to a discussion of the first of our historical cross sections (*c.* 1875), it is desirable to consider briefly the progress of survey and settlement in the example areas before this date. Prior to the coming of the white man, small numbers of Indians utilized the region and to some extent engaged in mound building. However, the Indians had an entirely different concept of land ownership than did the American settlers;[26] this light aboriginal land occupance has little relevance to this study. There are traditions of white men resident among the Indians both north and south of the Scioto before the real advance of the frontier.[27]

---

from Virginia in some localities in the Virginia Military District of Ohio, because of the transfer of titles to land, it was by no means exclusively an enclave of Virginians. This last statement is particularly true of the northern section of the District.

[26]Vernon Carstensen, *The Public Lands,* The University of Wisconsin Press, Madison, 1963, pp. xiii-xiv. In his introduction to this collection of essays on the various aspects of the public domain, Professor Carstensen brings out this essential difference in attitude. The Indian regarded land as the common property of all the inhabitants of an area, a concept diametrically opposed to the European traditions of the American colonists.

[27]Some of the most persistent stories repeated in the local literature concern these early contacts between whites and Indians. A Virginian named Jonathan Alder was reported to be living with the Indians in the locality of U some twenty years before the first permanent settlement was effected (Henry Cring, *Caldwell's Atlas of Madison County, Ohio,* 1875, p. 6). Similarly, in the area later to be systematically surveyed, there are reports of soldiers remaining to trade with the Indians after the War of 1812. This would be about seven years before the area was originally surveyed and, again, nearly twenty years before substantial white settlement.

ORIGINAL LAND SURVEY AND SETTLEMENT IN EXAMPLE AREA U

From manuscript records kept in the several county courthouses in the Virginia Military District, it is possible to trace accurately the progress of original land subdivision in this survey tract. These records take the form of a cartographic and verbal description of each survey unit in the county. The following entries affecting one such unit from example area U are representative but a good deal simpler than many:[28]

Acres	Name	Survey No.	Warrant No.	Deputy Surveyor	Assignee	Date
466²/₃	Obadiah Smith	4807	685 (part)	James Galloway	William Rector	1806

Survey No. 4807 for 466 ²/₃ acres

Surveyed for Obadiah Smith 466 ²/₃ acres of land on part of a Military Warrant No. 685 on Little Darby's Creek.

Beginning at a Red Oak and Bur Oak running N 6 E 260 poles, crossing the Creek at 80 poles passing the Southeast corner of William Heth's Survey No. 4946 at 20 poles with his line passing his Northeast corner at 180 poles to a Stake. Thence S 84 E 250 poles to three Ashes, two from one root; thence S 6 W 345 poles crossing the Creek at 325 poles, to two Hickories and a Bur Oak; thence N 67 W 260 poles, crossing a branch at 20 poles to the beginning.

Samuel Mitchell   James Galloway D. S.
William Townsley   May 20, 1806
   Robert Morrison M.   June 10, 1806

Patent for Survey No. 4807 for 466 ²/₃ acres

From   The United States of America
The United States of America   to all to whom these presents shall
         to   come, Greeting. Know ye that in con-
William Rector   sideration of military service per-
—————————————————   formed by Obadiah Smith (a Lieu-
tenant for three years) to the United States in the Virginia Line of Continental Establishment and in pursuance of an Act of the Congress of the United States passed on the 10th day of August, in the year 1790 entitled "An act to enable the officers and soldiers of the Virginia Line of Continental Establishment to obtain titles to certain lands lying

---

[28]The area of this survey is now in Union County and it was from manuscripts from the archives of this county, housed in the courthouse at Marysville, Ohio, that these reports were copied. Because it is a relatively simple quadrilateral, it will be appreciated that this description is uncomplicated (see Figure 8b of the present study for the location of this parcel of land). For complex descriptions of land in the Virginia Military District, see Peters, *op. cit.*, pp. 21-25 with accompanying plats.

Original Survey and Land Subdivision

6	5	4	3	2	1	6	5	4	3	2	1
7	8	9	10	11	12	7	8	9	10	11	12
18	17	16	15	14	13	18	17	16	15	14	13
19	20	21	22	23	24	19	20	21	22	23	24
30	29	28	27	26	25	30	29	28	27	26	25
31	32	33	34	35	36	31	32	33	34	35	36
6	5	4	3	2	1	6	5	4	3	2	1
7	8	9	10	11	12	7	8	9	10	11	12

ABOVE { ≡≡≡ AREA SURVEYED IN 1820 (UNSHADED AREA SURVEYED IN 1819)
        (EDUCATIONAL LANDS – SECTIONS NUMBERED 16)

BELOW { ░░░ AREA SURVEYED BY 1810 (UNSHADED AREA SURVEYED SUBSEQUENTLY)
        ～～ MAJOR STREAMS   ······ AREA COVERED BY FIGURES 9a & 9b
        4807 OBADIAH SMITH'S SURVEY, PART OF V.M.D. WARRANT 685

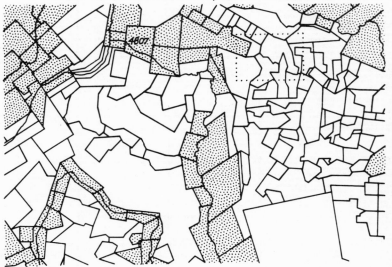

Figures 8a and 8b Progress of Original Survey in the Example Areas (S above and U below).

northwest of the River Ohio between the Little Miami and Sciota [*sic*] and another Act of the said Congress passed on the 9th day of June in the year 1794 amendatory of the said Act, there is granted by the said United States unto William Rector, Assignee of John H. Smith, who was Assignee of the said Obadiah Smith a certain tract of land containing four hundred and sixty six and two thirds acres, situate [*sic*] between the Little Miami and Sciota [*sic*] Rivers, northwest of the River Ohio as by Survey bearing date the twentieth day of May in the year one thousand eight hundred and six and bounded and described as follows: To Wit: Survey of four hundred and sixty six and two thirds acres of land on part of a Military Warrant No. 685 in favor of said Obadiah Smith (the whole thereof being for two thousand six hundred and sixty six and two thirds acres) on Little Darby's Creek. [Then follows description above].

To have and To hold the said tract of land with the appurtenances unto the said William Rector and his heirs and assignees forever.

In witness whereof the said James Madison, President of the United States of America hath caused the Seal of the United States to be hereunto affixed and signed the same with his hand at the City of Washington the twenty ninth day of June in the year of our Lord one thousand eight hundred and thirteen and of the independence of the United States of America, the thirty seventh.

By the President
James Madison

Seal

The earliest cadastral surveys undertaken in area U are dated 1798 but the most active period of original subdivision was the second decade of the last century (1810 to 1819). Nearly half of the numbered survey areas in U were laid out and recorded in this ten-year period, with 1815 being the modal year. Shading has been used to show those areas which had been subdivided by the end of 1810 in U on Figure 8b, from which it will be noticed that riparian sites were preferred by the earlier claimants, partly because it was easier to locate river-fronting lands. As long as surveys were confined to the rivers, a relatively simple pattern was produced, but it became increasingly complicated as latecomers fitted their claims in the interfluvial areas. In this fashion, all of the land in U had been transferred from public to private and local ownership by the year 1855 except for one small parcel of 7 acres. As in other survey districts, many transactions were made by surveyor-speculators, of whom James Galloway (previously noted) is one of about a dozen who, in total, disposed of the greater part of area U. During the early years of settlement an extremely fluid situation existed, with some numbered survey plots being parceled out almost immediately and taken up as properties.

Although a majority of the first white settlers in area U were from Virginia and Kentucky, soon pioneers from Pennsylvania, New York, and other states appeared. This locality later became more cosmopolitan than most areas of the District farther south, especially as these pioneers from northern states and a few foreign-born settlers purchased the land, the cost of which, initially, was as low as 80 cents per acre. Although there are certain obvious advantages in being near a stream, some of the best arable lands in the area are the interfluves which were generally settled last. By the middle of the century the area had become demographically mature, in the sense that its population at that time was not remarkably less than it is today and substantial increases and decreases, which might have taken place, did not occur. While certain fluctuations are evident in the decennial census returns, some townships have not experienced great changes in total population since that date (compare Appendices C and D). Nearly all of area U in 1810 was in Madison County, which had been established in that year; the county was diminished in size in 1818 and again in 1820, so that now the example area falls in three counties (as shown in Figure 7b).[29]

ORIGINAL LAND SURVEY AND SETTLEMENT IN EXAMPLE AREA S

A major obstacle retarding settlement in area S was the fact that under the Treaty of Greenville (1795), the claims of the Indians to the hunting rights in these lands were upheld. These rights were not extinguished until 1818, after which date the Indians

[29]Randolph Chandler Downes, "Evolution of Ohio County Boundaries," *Ohio Archaeological and Historical Quarterly,* Vol. 36, Columbus, 1927, pp. 341-477 (see especially pp. 385, 402-403, and 405-407).

were removed to the west;[30] there was considerable military activity in this general region during the War of 1812. Government surveyors began laying out the fundamental cadastral survey lines in 1819 and had completed their work in area S by the following year. From records kept in the State Capitol at Columbus and in the courthouses of the three counties over which example area S extends, we can ascertain details of the methods and the progress of these surveys. In this area the work was carefully carried out under the direction of the Deputy Surveyor, Charles Roberts. Following instructions, township boundaries were run first and in the following order: south, east, north, and west. Markers were set up, bearing trees noted, corrections made, and the section lines run in. Only after these operations were completed was the land legally available for sale, and in area S, buyers appeared rather slowly at first; the earliest date of sales is 1829, approximately a decade after the original subdivision. But almost all the land in S had been sold to private parties by 1836, about one-half of the sales being made in that year. Nearly 500 plots had been disposed of in area S at this time; these original, separate properties contained wholly or partly in area S were subdivisions of the sections, whole sections, or blocks of sections. The largest property, of 4 square miles — the equivalent of four sections — was held by a speculator.[31] The modal-sized holding was 80 acres ($\frac{1}{8}$ section, or half quarter-section as officially designated); over 200 of the plots were of this size. However, a greater amount of land was disposed of in quarter-sections, over a third of the land area of S being sold in

[30]Sherman, *op. cit.,* pp. 132-133. Although the final treaty with the Indians affecting Northwestern Ohio was not concluded until 1842, the area contained in example area S was available for white settlement at the end of 1818.
[31]Information on original sales of land in example area S was obtained from bound, unpublished manuscripts under the title, "Tract Book Entries, U. S. Land," from the office of the Auditor of State, Columbus, Ohio. These records and those kept in the county courthouses are often searched by attorneys and abstractors, since an abstract or certificate of title is necessary to secure a loan and for title insurance. Such a search is usually much more difficult in the Virginia Military District records. There was no upper limit to the size of original purchases of public land, but the lower limit (sometimes circumvented) was 80 acres, according to a law passed by Congress in 1820; the minimum amount was reduced to 40 acres in 1832 by an act implemented in 1834 (Donaldson, *op. cit.,* pp. 205, 214).

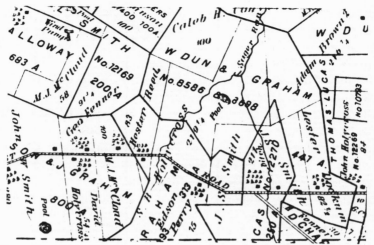

Figure 9a   Part of Example Area U from Darby Township Map Contained in Andrew S. Mowry, *Atlas of Union County, Ohio*, Philadelphia, 1877.

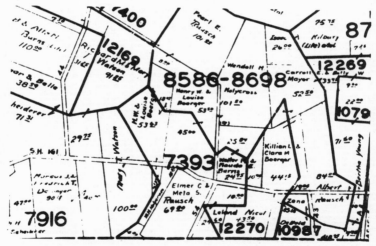

Figure 9b   The same area from a Modern Cadastral Map Compiled in the office of the County Surveyor, Union County, Ohio, 1955. In both cases the heavier lines indicate boundaries of the original, numbered Virginia Military District survey units and lighter lines, the limits of individual properties. Large type is used for the original survey units and lighter type for the properties. Note how in b the area of properties which straddle the original surveys is recorded in terms of the amount of land occurring in each of these basic units.

units of this size (160 acres). The plots still unsold in 1836 included the two sections numbered 16 in the area S; sections 16, according to the Ordinance of 1785, were reserved for educational purposes.[32] A detailed map of the original properties in S was constructed to facilitate research but this is not reproduced. There is little value in analyzing these distributions further because many of the original land purchases in area S were transitory. Some pioneers were interested only in fulfilling their government contracts and then moving on to new lands to the west. In comparison with those from the Virginia Military District, the entries for properties contained in the tract books of the systematically surveyed area are extremely simple. The following is the first such entry affecting example area S:

> Township 2S   Range XE   Section 2
> E ½ NE   acres
> W ½ NE   159.44; William Woodruff, June 1st, 1829.[33]

Most of the land in area S was sold at Bucyrus, Ohio, except the so-called Ohio Canal Lands in this locality, amounting to eighteen sections which were disposed of at the land office at Tiffin, Ohio.[34] The minimum "official" price was $1.25 per acre at this time, but much land in Northwestern Ohio fell into the hands of speculators who charged a higher figure. Some of the land was purchased by settlers who had had unhappy experiences in the Virginia Military District and had moved north. Practically all of the land in area S had been transferred to private ownership by the middle of the last century.

[32]*Journals of Congress, op. cit.*, Vol. 4, p. 521, and Donaldson, *op. cit.*, pp. 223-231. These school lands were sold later through the office of the Auditor of State, the revenue arising from these sales being used for educational purposes.

[33]From manuscript records as indicated in footnote 31 of this chapter. In contrast, the property descriptions of unsystematically surveyed properties sometimes occupy a full page of text and read rather like the description of V.M.D. Survey No. 4807, previously noted. Some of these unsystematic surveys close well (i.e., give a closed figure when plotted), but many do not and thus provide additional problems.

[34]Donaldson, *op. cit.*, pp. 257-258. Under a law dated May 24, 1828, Congress granted to the State of Ohio lands for the construction of canals. However, these lands thus donated by the United States to Ohio were bounded by lines of the rectangular surveys and were disposed of in the same manner and at approximately the same time as adjacent United States lands.

Having sketched the progress of survey, subdivision, and settlement to this point, we are now in a position, by means of geographical cross sections, to focus upon the effects of these developments in the example areas at two periods. Where necessary, the findings will be related to the larger framework of the survey district, the state, and the country. Indeed, the special value of these purposive samples is that they exemplify characteristics of a general nature. Various localities in Ohio and in other states including New York, Virginia, Kentucky, Wisconsin, and Iowa were studied and visited for the purpose of verifying the results of these investigations.

III.

Survey, Administrative, and Property Units in the
Example Areas, c. 1875

THE PERMANENT UNITS used as a frame of reference for locations, legal descriptions, and transfer of property in the systematically subdivided areas are the surveyed townships and sections. Likewise, in the Virginia Military District of Ohio the unchanging units are the original, numbered survey plots. Townships and sections have their special numbers (Figure 8); so also does each Virginia Military District survey unit have a unique number or series of numbers (Figures 9a and 9b). Although civil boundaries may change through time, and property and field lines are not permanent, the originally surveyed sections and the numbered survey units are intended to remain as standard areas in their respective districts.[1]

---

[1]County surveyors, lawyers, and land abstractors in the Virginia Military District of Ohio, in conversation with the writer, have all testified to the continuing importance of the original, numbered survey plots. Terms such as "indispensable" and "can't do without them" were used to describe these units. Those persons most concerned with land problems stressed the comparability of numbered plots for the District to the sections for the systematically surveyed areas. Accordingly, the original, numbered survey plots are a prominent feature of the V.M.D. township cadastral maps (both early and contemporary examples), as illustrated by Figures 9a and b. The numbers of the parcels of land are not noted on Figure 8b because of the difficulty of accommodating these in the smallest units of the map. However, survey unit 4807, which is described earlier in the text, is indicated by numbers on Figure 8b, and other numbered units for a small part of this map can be ascertained from Figure 9.

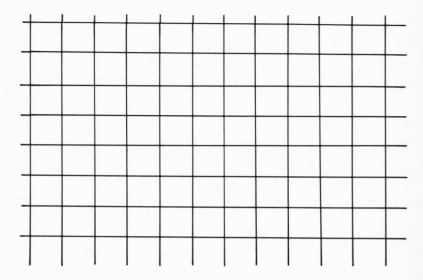

ABOVE ———— *SECTION LINES, EXAMPLE AREA S.*

BELOW ———— *NUMBERED SURVEY UNITS, EXAMPLE AREA U.*

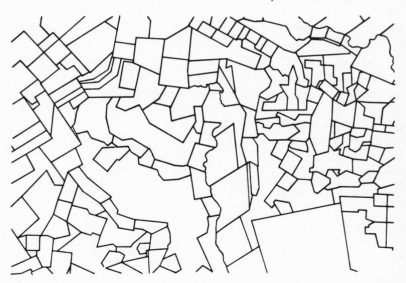

Figures 10a and 10b Basic Original Cadastral Survey Lines in the Example Areas.

NUMBERED SURVEY UNITS AND THE RECTANGULAR SECTIONS

A comparison between the arrangement of sections in example area S and the numbered survey units in example area U is provided by Figures 10a and 10b. These maps contain the same base information as Figures 8a and 8b, but because Figure 10 is unencumbered with overlay material and streams, which are not major survey boundaries (some streams which are not survey boundaries appear in 8b to illustrate riparian settlement), it permits a better comparison between the original survey units of the two areas. Basic units in U (Figure 10b) vary greatly with respect both to size and shape. A few of the units in this unsystematically surveyed area are square or rectangular, but most are not simple, regular geometrical figures. However, the boundaries are generally composed of straight lines because they were surveyed from point to point with the aid of the magnetic compass.[2] Where large streams occur, they usually serve as the boundaries of the numbered survey units, but some of these straddle considerable rivers (compare Figure 8b with Figure 10b). Narrow gores separate several of the larger numbered units, while other areas give the appearance of being fitted, as indeed they were, between more regularly shaped parcels of land. The complicated pattern shown in Figure 10b was developed following 1798, the year of the earliest property survey in U, and before 1871, when all lands not claimed in the Virginia Military District were ceded by the United States to the State of Ohio.[3] In example area U, only a

[2]Metes and bounds surveys, in which the lines are run with a magnetic compass, differ in detail from those cadastral surveys for which such an instrument was not employed. Thus there is an angular character to the lines of the true metes and bounds survey, no matter how unsystematic (indiscriminate) the over-all pattern, in contrast to the irregularity of the boundary lines of other types of unsystematic cadastral survey where the limits are often marked by a trail, hedgerow, dike, ditch, etc.

[3]Thomas Donaldson, *The Public Domain,* Government Printing Office, Washington, D.C., 1884, pp. 233-234. Both parts of Figure 10 have a common scale which, in turn, is the same scale as that of Figures 7a, 7b, 8a, and 8b. All of the maps which follow Figure 10 in this study (except those in the Appendices) also have this scale, as well as north orientation. It was considered unnecessary to repeat on each map scale and orientation information, for which the reader is referred to Figure 7.

few acres were affected by this statute, which like other such lands were given in 1872 by the state to the Ohio Agricultural and Mechanical College, now Ohio State University.

No accurate, general map of the fundamental survey units of the Virginia Military District has been made,[4] but in each county courthouse, survey records are available for public examination. Usually these records consist of a series of maps bound into volumes, one survey unit, characteristically, appearing on each page. Figure 10b was made by comparing a number of such sources. Where the numbered units straddle boundaries, especially, discrepancies exist; the records of the county in which the particular part of the parcel of land lies were used as the ultimate authority where there was nonagreement. No compilation difficulty of this kind was experienced when dealing with the area of systematic survey. Here, as shown on Figure 10a, subdivision is remarkably uniform. At the borders of the surveyed townships some of the lines are slightly offset, but by and large, township and section lines run in cardinal directions and enclose essentially mile-square plots of land in this example area (S).

In the matter of their size, as in their boundaries, a great contrast exists between the fundamental survey units of the Virginia Military District and those of the systematic surveys. Figure 11 is a graph in which all the units contained wholly or in part in the example areas S and U are arrayed to illustrate this factor of size. In spite of the minor irregularities of the systematic survey, the resulting sections are so close to 640 acres each that they appear as a straight line on the graph. There are 117 of these almost equal-sized sections contained wholly or in part in S. It should be mentioned that sections are not as accurately

[4]The best general representation of the various survey tracts of the state on a uniform scale is the "Map of Ohio showing Original Land Subdivisions," which accompanies the report of C. E. Sherman, *Original Ohio Land Subdivisions,* Final Report, Ohio Cooperative Topographic Survey, Columbus, 1925. This folded map of 6 inches to the mile (3 feet 6 inches x 3 feet 9 inches, approx.) is excellent considering the scale; nevertheless, Sherman himself recognized its limitations for showing all the details of subdivision. He also indicated that gaps in the record preclude the possibility of making a uniformly good map of all of the V.M.D. Sherman, *op. cit.,* p. 8 and p. 37.

delimited in all parts of the United States which are systematically surveyed as they are in Northwestern Ohio.[5]

In contrast to the uniformity of size of the sections of example area S is the size variation of numbered survey units in the Virginia Military District (example U). Such units, contained wholly or in part in this example area, range in size from almost 4,000 acres to less than 10 acres (Figure 11). The major reasons for gross differences in size of these parcels of land, i.e., military bounty according to rank and length of service and the method by which they were surveyed, assigned, and parceled out have already been indicated. Since the grants were characteristically for multiples of 100 acres, one may wonder why there are not more units at the 100-acre levels on the graph than are shown. There appear to be two major reasons for this: in the first place, there was no requirement that the whole of a particular grant be taken up as a contiguous tract (e.g., Obadiah Smith's grant, previously discussed) and, second, the areas enclosed are not necessarily for the amount specified in the warrant, even if taken up in one area, owing to inaccuracy of surveys or outright fraud.[6] Of the slightly more than 200 numbered survey units in U, only about 10 per cent exceed the size of the 640-acre sections with which they are compared. The most commonly occurring sizes are 100 acres (20 units) and 200 acres (10 units); these are the amounts, respectively, a private soldier and a noncommissioned officer would receive for less than three years service the most frequent rank and service combinations of the grantees. Within the limits of the example areas there are 195 miles of surveyed boundaries in S, as against 270 in U. Assuming equal conditions, the original subdividing, marking, mapping, and recording of fundamental survey units was a costlier job in area U than it was

---

[5]Jerome S. Higgins, *Subdivisions of the Public Lands*, St. Louis, 1887, pp. 121-138, illustration p. 134. This volume is an excellent example of literature designed to assist the government surveyor, the lawyer, and even the settler on matters related to the public lands.

[6]William E. Peters, *Ohio Lands and Their Subdivisions*, Athens, Ohio, 1918, p. 25 and p. 109. The amounts of land involved in the warrants ranged from 100 acres for a private soldier with less than three years of service to 15,000 acres for a major-general with four years of service. More land was required to fulfill these generous Virginia grants than for all of the other United States Revolutionary War land grants combined.

in area S. The relative effectiveness of these two contrasting methods of land subdivision in controlling future surveys will be treated subsequently. We are now in a position to consider the relationship between the fundamental survey lines and certain administrative boundaries.

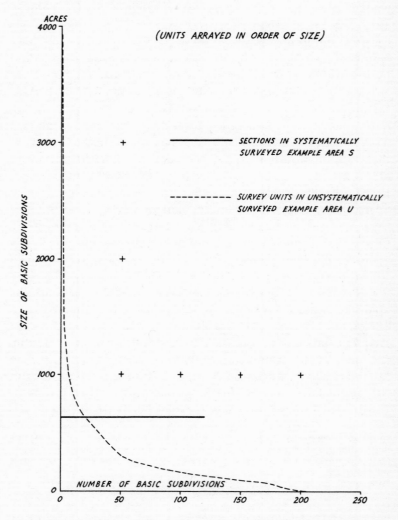

Figure 11   Number and Size of the Original Subdivisions in the Example Areas.

COUNTIES AND CIVIL TOWNSHIPS, C. 1875

Our first detailed historical cross section concerns the mid-1870's, about eighty years after the earliest sustained contact between the white man and the Indian in any part of the example areas. By 1875 both example areas had been settled for several decades and, as indicated previously, all land not claimed in U had been ceded by the federal government in 1871. Additional reasons for the choice of this period, following this last transfer of land from national to local control, are given in the next section of this chapter.

The first county division in the Northwest Territory took place in 1788,[7] and during the following one hundred years the arrangement of counties in Ohio essentially as we know it today was completed. All of the counties are, of course, now contained within state boundaries, but at the beginning of the last century some of them extended far beyond the present limits of Ohio.[8] From a very early date the unity of the Virginia Military District was shattered by county formation. The evolution of county boundaries in the state has been studied in detail[9] and we need not concern ourselves with this matter here, or, at present, with the county function. Our objective is to evaluate the relationship between administrative and cadastral survey lines in 1875.

The detailed situation with respect to the coincidence or lack of coincidence between civil division boundaries and the fundamental survey lines for the two example areas at the beginning of the last quarter of the nineteenth century is illustrated by Figures 12a and 12b. At that time there were about 20 miles of county boundaries in each of the two example areas. In S, surveyed township (and therefore section) lines coincided with

[7]Francis R. Aumann and Harvey Walker, *The Government and Administration of Ohio,* New York, 1956, pp. 430-453.

[8]Randolph Chandler Downes, "Evolution of Ohio County Boundaries," *Ohio Archaeological and Historical Quarterly,* Vol. 36, Columbus, 1927, pp. 340-477. See especially the maps in the early sections of this study.

[9]Downes, *loc. cit.* C. E. Sherman, writing in 1925 in *Original Ohio Land Subdivisions* (pp. 6-7), indicated that he had contemplated including in that work a series of maps showing the growth of Ohio counties but concluded that the topic demanded a separate treatment. Downes' work, which was published in 1927, is similar in form to studies for other states produced at about the same period and fills the gap noted by Sherman.

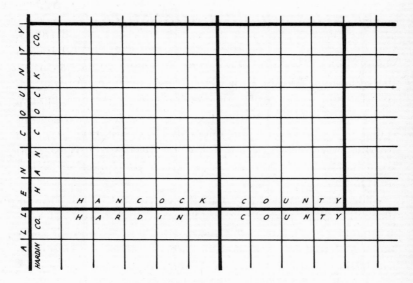

CIVIL BOUNDARY (COUNTY OR TOWNSHIP) AND FUNDAMENTAL
SURVEY LINE (SECTION, ABOVE ; V. M. D. UNIT, BELOW),
——————— COINCIDENT , • • • • • • NOT COINCIDENT.

Figures 12a and 12b Basic Survey Lines and Civil Boundaries in the
Example Areas.

county boundaries throughout the entire length of the county lines (Figure 12a). In contrast to this, no correspondence existed between original survey and county boundary lines in example area U (Figure 12b). Reasons for this difference, which as we shall see, significantly affects the lives of the people occupying the land, are not difficult to find. They relate to the original acts by which the counties were created and the implementation of these laws. The legal descriptions of county boundaries which were followed by the surveyors provide the key to an understanding of these differences. Union County, part of which is in example area U, and Hancock County partially in S were both created in 1820. The boundary descriptions of these two counties contained in the legislative reports of that year are given below. First, under the title "An Act to Erect the County of Union":

> ... beginning on the north boundary line of Delaware county on that part known by the name of the old Indian or Greenville line, at a point three miles west of the Scioto River, thence due south fifteen miles, thence east four miles, thence south unto the north boundary of Franklin county, thence two and one half miles into Franklin county, thence west to the east boundary of Madison county, and to continue west unto the east boundary of Champaign county, thence to the north east corner of said county, thence west three miles, thence north so far that a due east line will strike a point three miles north of the beginning, thence south to the said place of beginning. (Passed January 10, 1820.)[10]

No mention is made in this description, representative of others concerning Virginia Military District county limits, of the numbered survey units. These units existed, for the most part, before the county lines were surveyed; only a distance of about one mile of the county boundaries in U extended through areas not yet parceled out as original numbered survey plots in 1820. This general situation is typical of the District, where administrative boundaries usually bear no positive relationship to original survey lines; that there is any correspondence between these two sets of boundaries is explained, in some instances, by the fact that the numbered units were surveyed afterwards and were purposely terminated at county lines.

[10]*Acts of the State of Ohio,* Vol. 18, Columbus, 1820, pp. 56-57.

In contrast to the above, the descriptions of county boundaries in the area of rectangular surveys are generally made in terms of townships and sections and are thus "consequent" boundaries, rather than the typical "subsequent" county boundaries of the unsystematically surveyed areas. The boundaries of Hancock County (one of several counties created out of the Indian lands north of the Greenville Treaty Line) are described in the following manner:

> ... fifth, to include townships one and two south, and one and two north in the ninth, tenth, eleventh and twelfth ranges, and to be known by the name of Hancock. (Passed February 12, 1820.)[11]

Hancock County was diminished in size in 1845 by the formation of Wyandot County to the east, but the new boundary, which does not affect example area S, was again extended along original survey (township and section) lines. The simplicity of the Hancock County description in comparison with that of Union County is obvious; most of the counties in systematically surveyed Ohio have descriptions similar to that above. Indeed, the striking character of the political map of much of North America, with its prevailingly straight boundaries oriented in cardinal directions, can be explained largely in these terms.

Counties in the United States are commonly fragmented into smaller units known variously as minor civil divisions, towns, or as in the case of Ohio, townships. These townships have changed through time both in function and number. A legislative council of the Territorial Government ordered the creation, in 1790, of the first true Ohio civil townships.[12] Either "natural" or "determined" boundaries were permitted for these subdivisions of existing counties. In 1804 the state legislature directed that the entire state should be divided into civil townships.[13] Certain other aspects of the township will be treated later; now we shall focus our attention upon the relationship of minor civil division boundaries and cadastral survey lines in the example areas, *c.* 1875 (Figures 12a and 12b). The civil townships as they are shown on these maps were created between 1820 and 1850. No

[11]*Ibid.,* p. 90.

[12]James Alva Wilgus, "Evolution of Township Government in Ohio," *Annual Report of the American Historical Association,* Washington, D.C., 1895, pp. 403-412.

[13]Albert H. Rose, *Ohio Government, State and Local,* St. Louis, 1953, p. 24.

good purpose would be served by elaborating on the formation of these administrative units and the date of the erection of their boundaries, but it should be noted that in Ohio, surveyed and civil townships are not *necessarily* coincident in systematically surveyed areas. In other words, there is no legal requirement that the boundaries of these two types of township coincide, though as a matter of convenience they frequently do.

In 1875 there were in example area S slightly more than 25 miles of minor civil division boundaries (civil township lines) other than county boundaries, which are also always the limits of civil townships; in example area U the mileage was approximately the same. *Surveyed* township or section lines were used for the entire length of such boundaries in S. Actually all civil division boundaries in S are also surveyed township boundaries except the eastern margin of Van Buren Township, which extends along a section line to give that civil unit 24 instead of the usual 36 sections. By contrast to this complete correspondence between survey and civil lines, only about 3 miles of minor civil division and numbered survey unit boundaries were coincident in example area U (Figure 12b); half of this mileage is along stream courses. In systematically as in unsystematically surveyed Ohio, interior streams have not been used extensively as county boundaries, so that for these larger administrative units it may be said that such streams have been a unifying rather than a dividing factor.[14] However, the more important streams often serve as limits of townships, but this situation is more characteristic of the Virginia Military District as a whole than of systematically surveyed areas. (Compare maps, Appendices E and F).

As is evident from the map (Figure 12b), numbered survey units in the District in 1875 crossed civil division lines at any and all angles, so that one has the impression that had the authorities tried to avoid making the two sets of lines correspond, they could scarcely have succeeded better. Accordingly, the numbered survey units in U bordering civil boundaries are severed

[14]Although rivers have not formed a large share of the county boundaries *within* Ohio, more than half of the external or state boundaries (which are, of course, also county lines) extend along water bodies. Thus the southern and much of the eastern boundary of the state is marked by the Ohio River, while most of the northern boundary extends through Lake Erie.

by these boundaries into even more awkward-shaped patches of land. As shown on Figure 12b, one of these units falls partly in three townships, each of which is in a different county, and four townships of the same county each contain part of another unit. In 1875, about one-third of all the numbered survey units in example area U straddled county and township lines. Significant as this may be, after the settlement of the area the severance of numbered survey plots by civil boundaries became less critical than the severance of *properties* by the civil lines. However, since the fundamental survey units to some extent control the subdivision of land into properties, the two factors are not unrelated. An attempt will be made to measure the extent to which property and original survey lines conform in the example areas, the degree of severance of properties by civil division boundaries, and the size of properties.

PROPERTY BOUNDARIES IN EXAMPLE AREAS, C. 1875

The reconstruction of the cultural landscape of much of the United States, at least at one period and in certain characteristics, is made possible by the county atlases. These unique records of the location of property lines, public buildings and dwellings, roads, and other features were produced by private companies for sale to local patrons.[15] Fortunately, the two example areas are covered by county atlases of comparable quality produced in the relatively short period 1874 to 1880.[16] The availability of these source materials, an important consideration in the choice of the

[15]Norman J. W. Thrower, "The County Atlas of the United States," *Surveying and Mapping*, Vol. 21, No. 3, September, 1961, pp. 365-373.

[16]Henry Cring, *Caldwell's Atlas of Madison County, Ohio,* Condit, Ohio, 1875; G. A. Eberhart and C. J. Pearce, *Illustrated Historical Atlas of Hancock County, Ohio,* Philadelphia, 1880; H. G. Howland, *Atlas of Hardin County, Ohio,* Philadelphia, 1879; Andrew S. Mowry, *Atlas of Union County, Ohio,* Philadelphia, 1877; J. W. Starr and J. N. Headington, *Atlas of Champaign County, Ohio,* Urbana, Ohio, 1874; Robert H. Harrison, *Atlas of Allen County, Ohio,* Philadelphia, 1880. Some compilers of county atlases such as Andrew S. Mowry, noted above, were surveyors and civil engineers with distinguished professional reputations. Through his apprentices, Mowry influenced generations of surveyors, some of whom are still active in western and northern Ohio.

date of the cross section, permitted a reconstruction of certain landscape characteristics of this time.[17]

Property boundaries of the example areas as shown in the county atlases, *c.* 1875, were first considered. As illustrated by Figure 9a, township plats of these atlases record property location, size, limits, and ownership. Information on Figures 13a and 13b, which is taken from the county atlas township plats, shows boundaries of contiguous plots of land under the same ownership in the respective example areas. Contiguous plots of land under the same ownership as shown on cadastral maps are not necessarily the same as farm units in rural areas. For example, an agriculturalist may own only a part of the land he farms or, again, a big estate may be broken up into several farm units. However, a contiguous plot of land under the same ownership

[17]The county atlas is an American phenomenon. The first of these privately sponsored volumes appeared in 1861, but by the early years of the twentieth century the county atlas had been replaced by the simpler county plat book. Usually the county atlas is handsomely bound and follows a rather uniform format. First, general maps of the state and county appear, followed by detailed plats of each township. Frequently, brief county and township historical and biographical disquisitions are included, and liberally interspersed with the written and cartographic materials are pictures of patrons and their establishments (Figures 35a and b). Over 4,000 different county atlases and plat books, many of which were published by a relatively small number of companies, are noted in *A List of Geographical Atlases,* by Philip L. Phillips, U. S. Government Printing Office, 1909-1920 (4 vols.), and in *United States Atlases,* by Clara E. Le Gear, Library of Congress, 1950 and 1953 (2 vols.). Even these lists are not complete. The distribution of counties covered by these atlases seems to coincide with the prosperity of the farming area combined with a large number of landowners in a given county. Thus the Corn Belt is well represented, but the South has little coverage. The county atlas is a valuable and, perhaps, neglected source for historical-geographical studies. In spite of obvious deficiencies, this source material is often the only detailed record of many geographical aspects of certain areas that we possess for the second half of the nineteenth century. Cartographic information in the county atlases was frequently copied, in the first place, from official township cadastral maps which have rarely survived, and was supplemented by field observations. Since these volumes were purchased locally, gross errors in platting are not likely to have been tolerated. Perhaps the best proof of their continuing importance is that county surveyors and lawyers frequently refer to these atlases today in an attempt to establish facts of land ownership. It was the opinion of several officials that a reconstruction of earlier cultural landscape patterns of the type undertaken in this study would not be possible without the county atlases. In conversation, Professor H. Clifford Darby emphasized the potential value of these records for historical-geographical studies; perhaps it is permissible to regard these documents as being comparable, in their own way, to the records compiled by the Norman clerks in England during the eleventh century.

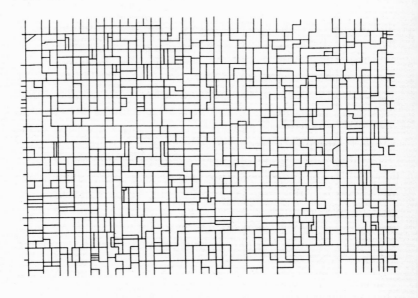

————— *PROPERTY BOUNDARIES IN THE EXAMPLE AREAS c. 1875*

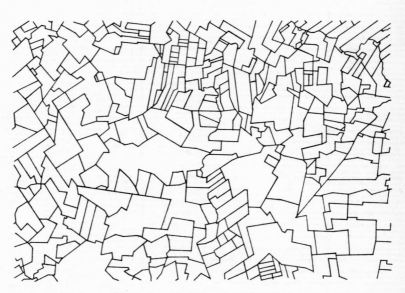

Figures 13a and 13b Property Boundaries in the Example Areas, *c.* 1875.

(individual, family, or corporation) in the example areas is usually the same as the commercial or noncommercial farm unit of the modern census report. Compared with the total, only an insignificant amount of land in both example areas was devoted to nonfarm uses, *c.* 1875; independent house lots, quarries, etc. have been excluded from the totals. A few cases of a proprietor owning two or more separated plots of land occur in both areas. These are treated as distinct units, but where lands under the same ownership are attached diagonally at one corner, they are considered as a single unit. In Figure 13, property boundaries in the example areas (*c.* 1875) only are shown; roads have been omitted as well as all other lines. Property boundaries in example area U (Figure 13b) extend in all directions and enclose areas of very unequal size. By contrast, almost all the property boundaries occurring in example S (Figure 13a) are oriented in cardinal directions; there is a much smaller range in the size of property units in this area than in U. The contrasting patterns of lines and shapes shown in the two parts of Figure 13 illustrate graphically the property situation in areas where very different original surveys were employed. In 1875 there were 384 miles of property boundaries in U, 520 in S. At this period the price of agricultural land without buildings had advanced to $30 an acre in both S and U.[18]

An attempt has been made to show (Figure 14) the relationship of fundamental survey lines and property boundaries, *c.* 1875. At this time a discontinuous skeleton of Virginia Military District numbered survey unit boundaries limited the properties. Actually, approximately 49 per cent (132 out of a possible 270 miles) of the survey unit boundaries delimited properties; the remainder (51 per cent of these lines) ran through, rather than around individual holdings (Figure 14b). Only two properties were coextensive with the original numbered survey parcels at this time, although some large estates included more than one whole unit of this kind. Large estates in 1875 tended to

[18]From manuscript records of land transfers at this period, summarized from a large number of transactions recorded in deed books available for study in the courthouses of the counties concerned, and from conversations with lawyers, farmers, and local officials.

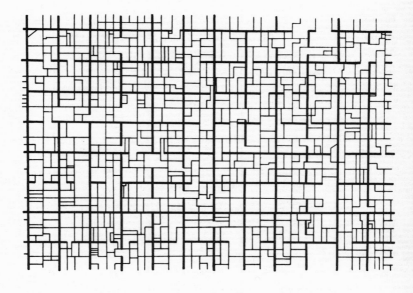

FUNDAMENTAL SURVEY LINES (SECTIONS, ABOVE; V.M.D. UNITS, BELOW) AND PROPERTY BOUNDARIES COINCIDENT c. 1875.

Figures 14a and 14b Relationship of Fundamental Survey Lines and Property Boundaries in the Example Areas, *c.* 1875.

be located in the areas of large original survey tracts; small properties of the time were carved out of both large and small numbered survey parcels. Some of the more "unreasonable" original subdivision lines were not retained as property boundaries, although it must be admitted that many of the property boundaries in 1875 themselves enclosed awkward-shaped patches of land.

As shown in Figure 14a, almost all section lines of example area S served as property boundaries *c.* 1875; out of a total of 195 miles of section lines, 177 (91 per cent) divided one property from another. In both example area U and example area S, fundamental survey lines served as guides and points of departure for further subdivision even where they may not actually have been used as boundaries. This control is much stronger in the systematically surveyed area S where, in 1875, only about .02 per cent of property lines were not oriented in the same cardinal directions as the original fundamental survey lines.

In the matter of the size and shape of properties and the orientation of boundaries, great contrasts existed between example areas S and U, *c.* 1875. The sizes of all properties contained wholly or in part in the example areas were considered; therefore, in each case an area in excess of 64,000 acres (100 square miles) was included, but in neither case did it exceed 70,000 acres. As shown on the graph (Figure 15), there were, in 1875, well over twice as many individual properties in example area S as in area U (712 against 305); on the graph all individually owned contiguous properties are plotted according to size for example areas S and U. The range in size of these units was much greater in U (1,900 to less than 10 acres) than in S (640 to less than 10 acres). The average size of a property in U was about 230 acres, in S, 90 acres. There was no special predominance of properties in any particular size category in U in 1875; it was quite otherwise in S. The largest number of properties of one size in U was 9 at 100 acres each. In contrast, example area S presents a multi-modal situation with 65 properties at 160 acres (¼ section), 200 at 80 acres (⅛ section), and 120 at 40 acres (¹⁄₁₆ section). It is no accident that the great majority of all the properties in example area S are simple proportions of a section, for these were the most common units involved in the original transfer of land from public to private ownership and served as convenient units for subsequent legal changes of title. The plateau-like nature of property sizes in S on this graph stands in contrast to the rather smooth curve made by plotted property sizes in U.

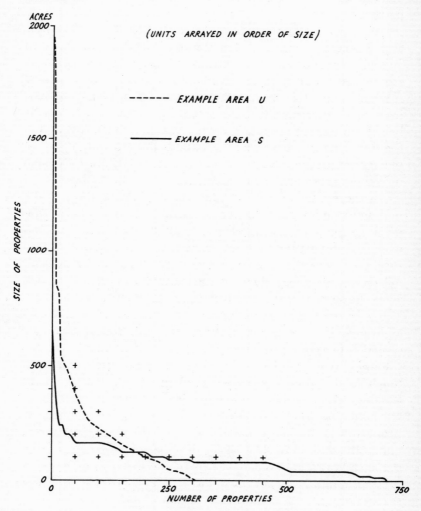

Figure 15   Number and Size of Properties in the Example Areas, *c.* 1875.

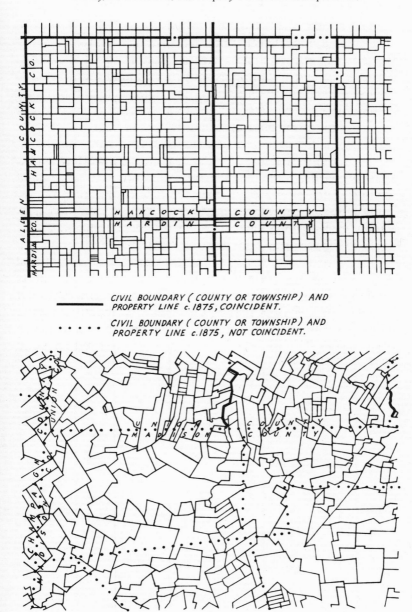

CIVIL BOUNDARY (COUNTY OR TOWNSHIP) AND PROPERTY LINE c. 1875, COINCIDENT.

CIVIL BOUNDARY (COUNTY OR TOWNSHIP) AND PROPERTY LINE c.1875, NOT COINCIDENT.

Figures 16a and 16b Relationship of Property and Civil Division Boundaries in the Example Areas, *c.* 1875.

The relationship of these property boundaries of 1875 to civil division lines reflects this same characteristic for the more fundamental survey units, viz., the relationship of numbered survey units and section lines with civil boundaries, previously discussed. Figure 16 illustrates the relationship of property boundaries and civil lines of the two areas, *c.* 1875. At this date no property terminated at a county line in example area U; properties at the periphery of counties were partly contained in two or even three counties. Similarly, along the township boundaries, properties commonly extended into two or more of these minor civil divisions. About 3 miles of civil township and property boundaries were coincident in U (Figure 16b). Most of this correspondence was along lines where the original numbered survey unit and the township boundaries coincided. By contrast, in the rectangularly surveyed area, in 1875, it was clearly exceptional for properties to cross civil boundaries. Thus not one property straddled a county line in S, and only five properties straddled township lines at this period for a total of slightly under 2 miles. We can now turn to the contemporary situation with respect to matters discussed above and other related phenomena.

IV.

Property, Survey, and Administrative
Units in the Example Areas, c. 1955

IN THE PREVIOUS CHAPTER, some factors respecting original survey, administrative, and property units and their interrelationship were considered. For this purpose small examples were used, permitting an analysis of various detailed characteristics which, within certain limits, are representative of larger areas of contrasting cadastral surveys. The same example areas will be examined in this chapter for the purpose of studying the present character of these and other units and evaluating effects upon the landscape of settlement between 1875 and 1955.

Field work for this study was begun in 1955, and uniform statistical and cartographic records were collected at that time. There is no compelling necessity to bring an historical, geographical study up to date,[1] but in fact the areas were revisited and examined several times after 1955. Between that date and the early 1960's only minor differences were noted. The situation in 1955, eighty years after the cross section discussed in the

---

[1]Preston E. James and Clarence F. Jones (Editors), *American Geography, Inventory and Prospect*, Syracuse, 1954, pp. 70-105. These problems are discussed in Chapter 3 of this volume by Andrew Clark who states, "The rationale of historical geography is that through its study we may be able to find more complete and better answers to the problems of interpretation of the world both as it is now and as it has been at different times in the past," p. 95. As an example of a study which fits the latter part of this statement, Ralph H. Brown's *Mirror for Americans, Likeness of the Eastern Seaboard, 1810,* American Geographical Society, New York, 1943, might be cited.

previous chapter and approximately double that time from the first sustained contact between the American settlers and the Indians in the area, can be taken as representative of contemporary conditions. The various areal units will be discussed in the order which, it is believed, best brings out characteristics important for this study.

PROPERTY AND SURVEY UNITS

Even if it were feasible to trace in detail all of the changes in property boundaries in the example areas at several different periods between 1875 and the present time, it would seem unnecessary to do this; indeed there would be a diminishing return in producing a large number of historical cross sections.[2] Information on contemporary property boundaries in rural Ohio is available from the county engineer responsible for the area. "The county engineer must keep a record of all surveys made for the purpose of locating any land or road lines, which record is open to inspection in his office at any time. . . ."[3] Usually the record is in the form of large-scale township maps which are amended as property titles and boundaries change. Because the original maps are constantly being brought up to date and because copies are not required to be deposited in the county archives at specified intervals, there is no permanent over-all cartographic record of the property boundaries at any given time, except the present. Since, in a sense, these are self-liquidating records, one is normally limited to a consideration of the contemporary situation. Figure 9b is a somewhat reduced copy of a small part of one of these township maps and illustrates the general character of this cartographic genre.

The arrangement of property lines over the whole of exam-

[2]Complete coverage by cadastral maps of areas S and U is contained in plat books of the counties concerned, prepared at unspecified dates by W. H. Hixson of Rockford, Illinois. These plat books are indicated in Clara E. Le Gear, *United States Atlases,* Library of Congress, 1950 and 1953, 2 vols., as being published in "[19--]." Communications with the publisher and other investigations failed to produce a more precise dating of these documents. Hence, though consulted, they were not used as fundamental source materials for this study.

[3]Albert H. Rose, *Ohio Government, State and Local,* St. Louis, 1953, p. 59.

ple areas S and U, in 1955, is illustrated in Figure 17. This information, which was compiled from official plats of the 18 townships in the 6 counties involved in the example areas, is greatly reduced in scale from the original maps. The same definition of a property (i.e., a contiguous plot of land under the same ownership) was used when constructing Figure 17 as for maps showing property boundaries, *c.* 1875 (Figure 13). As in the previous case, *only* property lines are shown on the two parts of the map.

Figure 17b illustrates that the present landscape of example area U is one containing properties of varied shape and size with unsystematically oriented boundaries. In its gross pattern, with large parcels of land in the area where they were located in 1875, this property situation of 1955 resembles that prevailing eighty years earlier (compare Figure 13b with Figure 17b).[4] Similarly, the character of the boundaries and the sizes and shapes of properties in rectangular example S (Figure 17a) at present generally follow the pattern in this area of an earlier period (Figure 13a).

An attempt was made to measure the magnitude of the change in the respective example areas between 1875 and 1955. The extent to which the unchanging fundamental survey lines (e.g., numbered survey unit or section lines) serve as present-day property boundaries is an indication of the degree of control exercised by these lines (Figure 18). In example area U, 117 out of a total of 270 miles of Virginia Military survey unit boundary lines coincided with property lines in 1955. This is approximately 44 per cent of survey unit boundary lines serving as property boundaries, as opposed to 49 per cent (132 miles out of 270) serving this purpose in 1875. Although there is less total mileage of survey unit and property boundaries in U coinciding today than eighty years ago, not all the same lines were involved then and now. The net loss in coincidence of original survey unit and property lines between 1875 and 1955 was 15 miles, but 25

[4]Merle Prunty, Jr., "The Renaissance of the Southern Plantation," *Geographical Review,* 1955, Vol. 45, pp. 459-491. The persistence of large landholdings in the face of changing social and economic conditions is one of the main themes of this study.

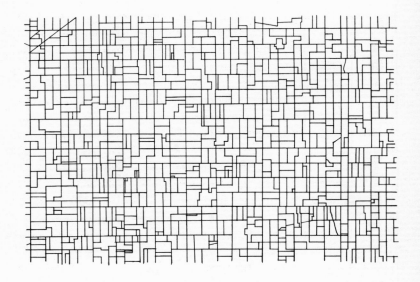

———— PROPERTY BOUNDARIES IN THE EXAMPLE AREAS c.1955

Figures 17a and 17b Property Boundaries in the Example Areas, *c.* 1955.

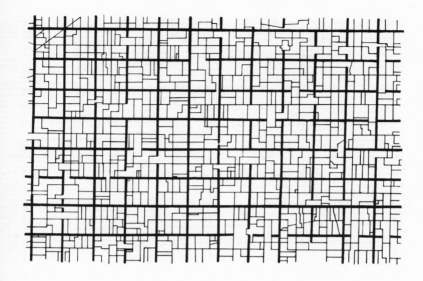

FUNDAMENTAL *SURVEY LINE (SECTION, ABOVE ; V.M.D. UNIT BELOW) AND PROPERTY BOUNDARY COINCIDENT, c. 1955.*

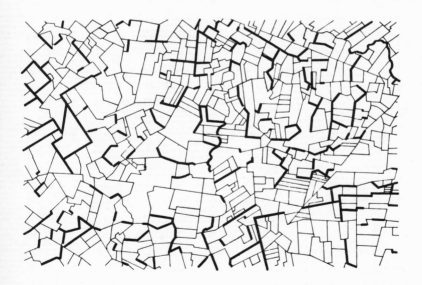

Figures 18a and 18b Relationship of Fundamental Survey Lines and Property Boundaries in the Example Areas, *c.* 1955.

miles (9 per cent) of survey unit boundaries were abandoned as property lines and 10 miles (4 per cent), not used as property boundaries at the earlier date, were "exhumed" and serve this purpose today. This illustrates the vitality and usefulness of the original survey unit lines, however unsystematic, in the subdivision description and transfer of property.

In contrast to the over-all loss in coincidence of property and fundamental survey lines in U is the situation in example area S. In this systematically surveyed area there is more coincidence between property and section lines now than at an earlier date. In 1955, 180 out of a total of 195 miles of section lines (92 per cent) served as property boundaries, whereas in 1875, 177 miles of section lines (91 per cent) coincided with property lines. Again, not all the section lines serving as property boundaries at the earlier date perform this function at the present time. Seven miles of section lines that were serving as property boundaries in 1875 (4 per cent of section lines in S) were not used for this purpose in 1955. However, 10 miles (approximately 5 per cent) of section lines not used as property lines in 1875 were so employed in 1955. This is a net gain of 3 miles (less than 2 per cent). While 128 miles (47 per cent) of basic survey unit boundaries in example area U served as property lines neither in 1875 nor in 1955, only 8 miles (approximately 4 per cent) of section lines were not used in this way at either of the two dates in example area S. Figures in the paragraphs above are presented in Table 1.

The stability of property boundaries is perhaps best expressed in terms of the property boundaries themselves, and Figure 19 attempts to illustrate this characteristic for the two example areas. Between 1875 and 1955 there was not a remarkable difference in the *percentage* of increase in the total length of property boundaries in the two example areas. In U, the total length of property boundaries had increased from 384 miles in 1875 to 444 miles in 1955, or an increase of approximately 16 per cent; the comparable figures for example area S rose from 520 to 592 miles, or an increase of about 14 per cent between the earlier and later date. Here the similarity ends. Out

TABLE 1

COINCIDENCE OF FUNDAMENTAL SURVEY AND
PROPERTY BOUNDARIES, C. 1875 AND C. 1955
Total section line boundaries, Area S 195 miles (100%)
Total survey unit boundaries, Area U 270 miles (100%)

Area	1875	1955	1875 not 1955	1955 not 1875	Neither 1875 nor 1955
S					
Miles	177	180	7	10	8
Per cent	91	92	4	5	4
U					
Miles	132	117	25	10	128
Per cent	49	44	9	4	47

(All figures rounded)

of the total of 444 miles of property boundaries in example area U in 1955, 186 miles (42 per cent) were the same lines as in 1875 (Figure 19b). In contrast, out of the 592 miles of property boundaries in S in 1955, 463 miles (about 78 per cent) were the same as eighty years earlier (Figure 19a). Naturally there was also some abandonment of property boundaries between 1875 and 1955 in the two example areas. This was due to the transfer of property from one owner to another, through consolidation and attendant boundary adjustments.[5] In area U, 198 miles of property lines were abandoned between 1875 and 1955, or 45 per cent of the total property boundaries at the later date. In contrast, only 57 miles of property lines were abandoned in area S between 1875 and 1955, or 10 per cent of the total property boundaries of 1955. Not only was there more abandonment of property lines in area U between the two dates, there was also more mileage added to this area. Thus, altogether, 258 miles of new property boundaries were added in U between 1875 and 1955, or 58 per cent of the total property lines of the later date (Figure 19b). Only 129 miles of new property boundaries were

[5]These transactions are recorded on a Certificate for Transfer of Real Estate which is sent for filing to the Recorder of the county in which the property is located. These instruments are commonly signed by a Probate Judge and a Deputy Clerk, as well as the Recorder. Information supplied by Lawrence B. Rhoads, Recorder, Union County, who showed the writer examples of these transfers.

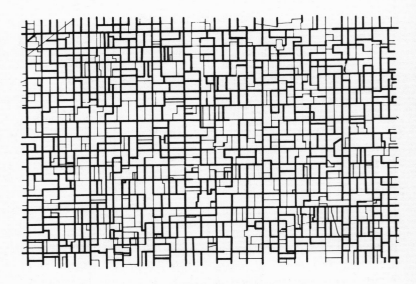

——————— PROPERTY LINE c.1875 SERVING AS A PROPERTY LINE c.1955.

(HEAVY AND LIGHT LINES, TOGETHER REPRESENT PROPERTY LIMITS c.1955)

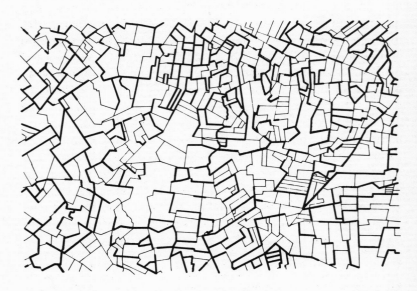

Figures 19a and 19b Property Boundaries of *c.* 1875 Serving as Property Boundaries *c.* 1955 in the Example Areas.

added in S in the eighty-year period, or 22 per cent of all property lines of 1955 (Figure 19a). All these processes go on rather evenly over the respective areas.

The conclusion to be drawn from the figures is inescapable: there is much more fluidity of property boundaries in the unsystematically surveyed Virginia Military District area than under the rigid framework provided by the rectangular section lines of the systematically surveyed area. It is not difficult to appreciate, after considering these changes, why there has been more litigation concerning property boundaries in the Virginia Military District (one-sixth of the land area of Ohio) than in all the rest of the state.[6] Figures in the paragraphs above are summarized in Table 2.

Certain aspects of property boundary changes are illustrated by Figures 19a and 19b. However, these changes cannot be properly understood until the resulting subdivision of the land in terms of the number and size of units and in respect to the transportation network are considered. The former matter will be examined now and the latter in a subsequent chapter.

In 1875, as previously demonstrated, example area U contained properties of very unequal size, while those of S deviated much less from a norm. These statements are generally true of the respective areas today in spite of some tendency toward equalization between U and S. There are considerably more individually owned properties now in both areas than there were eighty years ago. In 1955, as shown on the graph (Figure 20), there were 465 properties in U as against 875 in S. This represents an increase of 23 per cent in S (712 properties in 1875) and 52 per cent in U (305 properties in 1875). If division of land into properties had progressed in area S at the same rate as in area U, there would be over 1,000 properties in S today instead of 875. To the extent that there is proportionately less difference in the number of properties in 1955 than in 1875, there has been, between U and S, a degree of equalization in this factor. Actually, the differences in the total number of properties in the example areas between the two dates is approximately the same, just over 400 in 1875 and about the same number in 1955. There is little

[6]William E. Peters, *Ohio Lands and Their Subdivisions*, Athens, Ohio, 1918, p. 25.

TABLE 2

STABILITY OF PROPERTY BOUNDARIES BETWEEN C. 1875 AND C. 1955

Area	Total Mileage in		Increase 1955 over 1875		Per cent of 1955	Unchanged 1875 and 1955		Added between 1875 and 1955		Abandoned 1875 and 1955	
	1875	1955	Miles	Per cent		Miles	Per cent	Miles	Per cent	Miles	Per cent
S	520	592	72	14	12	463	78	129	22	57	10
U	384	444	60	16	14	186	42	258	58	198	45

(All figures rounded)

difference in the net increase of miles of boundaries added to create the new properties in the two example areas: 60 miles in U for 160 new properties; for about the same number of new properties in S, 72 miles (see Table 2).

The complex matter of the relation of length of boundary to shape and size of properties was investigated for the example areas. This matter has real significance, in respect not only to surveying costs but also to fence construction and repair, etc. A given geometrical figure of a small size has, of course, in proportion to its size a greater length of boundaries than a larger figure of the same shape. Thus a square plot of 40 acres has 1 mile of boundaries, while a 160-acre square plot (four times the area) has only 2 miles of boundaries. The geometrical figure which has the shortest boundary in relation to its area is the circle, but the figure most economical in boundary length, and which at the same time in combination with like-shaped figures takes up all the area of a given space, is the hexagon (honeycomb cells). In relation to its area, the square is less economical in length of

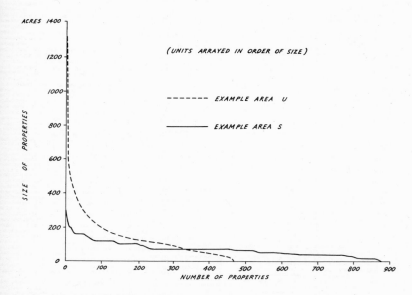

Figure 20 Number and Size of Properties in the Example Areas, *c.* 1955.

boundary than the hexagon; the oblong less than the square.[7] The most commonly occurring property shape and size combination in the S area is the 8o-acre plot, ½ x ¼ mile (oblong). A property of this size and shape has 7,920 feet of boundary, against about 7,467 feet for a square-shaped property of 80 acres. Because so many properties in the systematically surveyed area are oblong, and because some properties in the unsystematically surveyed area approach the economical hexagon shape (while others are very uneconomical in respect to their boundaries), there appears to be little difference in the over-all economy of property lines in relation to area in S and U. In both areas, in particular cases, there is certainly a great deal of difference.

The average size of properties in U, in 1955, was approximately 150 acres, in S, 70 acres; this is in contrast to 230 and 90 acres, the average figures, respectively, of the two example areas eighty years ago. Today the average-sized property in U is just over twice as large as that in S; in 1875 the average-sized U property was over two-and-a-half times as big as the average-sized S property of that date. Thus there has been some equalization in the average size of properties in S and U, as in other factors, over an eighty-year period. However, averages of property size as well as size classes (the principal ways they appear in the census) may conceal, rather than reveal, specific characteristics. Accordingly, consideration was taken of the sizes of all

[7]Although the circle is the geometrical figure with the shortest boundary in relation to its area, a continuous network of circles or ellipses cannot be developed on a plane surface in such a manner that all of the surface is covered by these figures without overlap or residue. The geometrical figure most economical in boundary length, which at the same time takes up all the area of a given plane surface, is the hexagon. The square is less economical than the hexagon, but has some obvious advantages for other reasons. Thus squares can be more readily subdivided into regular-shaped parcels of land suitable for agricultural purposes. A rectangular road network along the gridiron section lines is more reasonable than that developed around the boundaries of a continuous series of hexagons. Also the outer boundary of a block of rectangles can be a much simpler figure than the outer limits of a block of hexagons. In terms of length of boundary to a given area, the oblong (rectangle) is less economical than the square. Most of the properties in example area S are oblong-shaped parcels of land of various proportions. The approximate length of the boundaries of particular geometrical figures, each with an area of 1 square mile, is as follows: circle, 3.1 miles; hexagon, 3.7 miles; square, 4 miles; and an oblong (2 x 1), 4.2 miles.

properties contained wholly or in part in the example areas in 1955, as it was for 1875.

The results of this investigation are shown, in part, in graph form (Figure 20). The range in the size of properties in 1955 was much greater in U than in S, as was the case in 1875. The largest property in U today is 1,300 acres (by no means the largest property in the whole of the Virginia Military District), and the smallest less than 10 acres. In contrast, properties range in size from 320 acres (½ section) to less than 10 acres in S.

There were 24 properties of 100 acres each in example U in 1955; this is by far the largest number in any particular size category in this example area. As illustrated on the graph, properties in U, arrayed in order of size, grade rather evenly from size to size, producing a smooth curve (Figure 20). In contrast, the step- or plateau-like character of properties in S, arrayed in order of size, is as evident in the graph of the contemporary situation as it was in the graph showing sizes of properties in 1875 (Figures 15 and 20). In 1955, in S there were 25 properties of approximately 160 acres each (¼ section), 40 at 120 acres (³/₁₆ section), over 200 at 80 acres (⅛ section), 50 at 60 acres (³/₃₂ section), 120 at 40 acres (¹/₁₆ section), and 35 at 20 acres each (¹/₃₂ section). Properties of these sizes, simple divisions of the section, together account for an overwhelmingly large share of the land area of example S now, as they did in 1875. The "eighty" is still the most commonly occurring property size today in the systematically sudivided example area, as it was eighty years ago. The price of the land without buildings has now advanced to an average of $250 per acre in both of the example areas.[8]

COUNTIES, CIVIL TOWNSHIPS, AND PROPERTIES

The county and civil township boundaries in the two example areas, S and U, have remained unchanged for over a century

[8]According to the best available records, the average price per acre of purely agricultural land in this general region has fluctuated in recent decades from $150 in 1920, to $50 during the depression in 1930, to $250 in 1955 (dollars rounded).

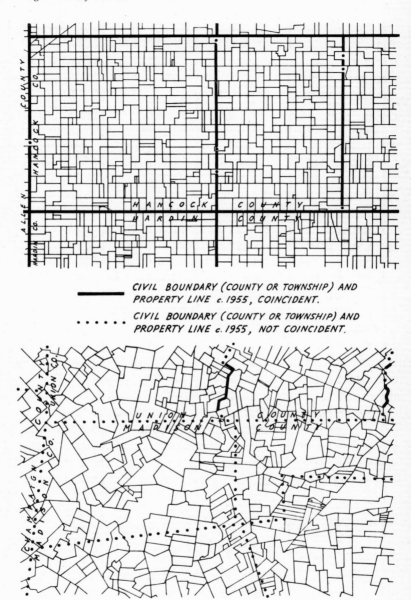

Figures 21a and 21b Relationship of Property and Civil Division Boundaries in the Example Areas, *c.* 1955.

and are today as indicated in Figures 7, 12, and 16. The relationship between county and civil township boundaries and the unchanging fundamental survey units, accordingly, is the same now as at the earlier period and need not be repeated.

Changes in property lines which took place between 1875 and 1955 did not materially alter the basic relationship between this class of boundary and the county lines. As shown before, in this characteristic the systematically and unsystematically surveyed areas offer almost the greatest possible contrast. In 1875 there was no coincidence between property and county boundaries; in other words, all county lines severed or bisected properties in example U; the same situation applies today (Figure 21b). Conversely, in example area S in 1875 all properties were contained within the county lines, while in 1955 practically the same condition obtained, with only one property straddling a county line for a total distance of $\frac{1}{8}$ mile (Figure 21a).

Today, as in earlier periods, the county is a most important administrative unit in rural, agricultural America. Other administrative units are frequently coextensive with the county or consist of blocks of these civil divisions. It is appropriate, therefore, to discuss briefly certain attributes of the county, since a consideration of these administrative units is necessary for an understanding of other matters to be considered later. These remarks apply particularly to Ohio counties as developed at present, hence the introduction of the discussion at this point; but some of the ideas expressed have wide application in the United States.

As mentioned earlier, the unity and cohesiveness of the Virginia Military District were soon destroyed by the creation of counties; only very small parts of the limits of this survey tract serve as county boundaries at the present time. In the development of Ohio counties, through the years, some of the major survey area boundaries of the systematically subdivided tracts have been coextensive with county lines to a much greater extent than is true in the case of the Virginia Military District. There are now 88 counties in Ohio; the boundaries of these administrative divisions and the limits of major survey tracts in the state are plotted together on the map, Appendix E. While only fragments of the limits of major survey tract boundaries are preserved as present-day county boundaries in Ohio, most of these county boundaries are surveyed township or section lines. This situation is reflected in the map of counties of the state where most of the internal boundaries in the systematically surveyed area are oriented essentially north-south and east-west. A deviation from these cardinal directions is more evident in the Virginia Military District, especially in those few counties contained entirely within this major survey tract.

The function of the Ohio county, like its boundaries, has changed through time; county government, which was at first very simple, is now complex.[9] County government has been much criticized, and proposals for reform have been suggested. Albert Rose summarizes the situation in these terms:

> Geographically, Ohio counties were laid out to fit the needs of early nineteenth century agricultural life . . .
> In general, urban counties have been increasing rapidly in population and rural counties declining or remaining stationary. Some 25 counties have fallen so much below the average of the state in per capita tax valuation as to have great difficulty in financing present day standards of local government.[10]

The need for a more "natural" unit than the county for certain purposes is expresed by the formation in Ohio of conservancy districts; 15 of these divisions are either functioning or proposed in the state. Conservancy districts embrace major streams and their tributaries, and the boundaries generally run along civil boundaries (county or township) close to the divide. Ohio Senatorial districts are formed of counties or blocks of counties. United States Congressional districts consist of counties or blocks of counties except in those cases where, because of the presence of a large population, it is necessary to subdivide the county. Further discussion of the significance of these county divisions

[9]Francis R. Aumann and Harvey Walker, *The Government and Administration of Ohio,* New York, 1956, pp. 437-445. Most of the work of the county government today is concerned with public welfare, public works, law enforcement, finance, and recording. Elected officials are responsible for each of these functions but are accountable to no executive head. The center of county administration is the county courthouse (Figure 36b).

[10]Rose, *op. cit.*, p. 48.

will be deferred until we have considered the civil townships (minor civil divisions) into which they are divided.

Just as the counties in Ohio are more than mere statistical units, so also are the civil townships. These minor civil divisions, like the counties of which they are a part, have changed through time both in function and number.[11] The total number of such divisions has declined from a peak of over 1,400 to about 1,300; some civil townships have been subsumed by expanding municipalities. The boundary of a civil township may be changed by the county commissioners on petition from a majority of the householders in the affected area.[12] From time to time state legislative directives have been issued concerning the minimum size of civil townships; at present no change may be made if it leaves one of these units with less than 21 square miles, although a smaller size was allowed previously and some examples of townships smaller than this survive in Ohio today. As in the county, elected officials are now responsible for the administration of the civil township.[13] Like the county, the civil township system has been attacked by critics who feel that the fragmentation of the state into many small administrative units is archaic and uneconomical. These charges are countered by the Ohio Association of Township Trustees and Clerks, which maintains that certain administrative duties are best performed at the local level. This Association, which was constituted in 1928 to safeguard the rights of the civil township official, is now one of the most influential groups in Ohio.[14]

The differences in the county boundaries of the unsystematically surveyed Virginia Military District and those of the counties within the systematically surveyed parts of Ohio are discernible,

---

[11]James Alva Wilgus, "Evolution of Township Government in Ohio," *Annual Report of the American Historical Association*, Washington, D.C., 1895, pp. 403-412.
[12]Rose, *op. cit.*, pp. 25-26.
[13]Aumann and Walker, *op. cit.*, pp. 450-451. The township, through its trustees, may buy or sell land, order the erection of certain public buildings and lay out parks and cemeteries. Other powers vested in the township officials include zoning regulations, preservation of the peace, and the maintenance of township roads. Some implications of the last of these duties will be indicated in the following chapter of this study dealing with roads and survey lines.
[14]Rose, *op. cit.*, pp. 43-44. The Township Clerks and Trustees each receive a small stipend and expense monies.

but not obvious, on a general map of the state. However, the civil township boundaries much more strongly reflect the basic cadastral survey system whether unsystematic or systematic (see map, Appendix F). Civil townships are generally rectangular in shape in the systematically surveyed tracts, in contrast to the irregularly shaped township units of most of the Virginia Military District. Counties which straddle the boundary between these two contrasting types of land subdivision generally include civil townships reflecting the character of the survey in which they are located. However, in some counties partly in a rectangular survey tract and partly in the Virginia Military District, the straight, consistently oriented lines of the civil townships of the rectangular area are carried across into the unsystematically surveyed parts of the county. Counties entirely in the Virginia Military District contain townships with boundaries characteristically possessing no dominant direction of orientation and frequently with quite irregular limits, except where coterminous with straight limits of the counties themselves. As previously indicated, only fragments of the major original survey district boundaries of Ohio are preserved in present county boundaries. A much more complete skeleton of these major survey district boundaries remains in contemporary civil township lines in the state. The limits of various minor survey districts are also evident as civil township lines, as well as historically important boundaries such as the Greenville Treaty Line (compare maps, Appendices E and F).

In the systematically surveyed parts of Ohio, most civil township boundaries are lines originally run for the purpose of subdividing land for sale and settlement. Approximately half of the civil townships in the rural parts of the state, outside of the Virginia Military District, are coincident with *surveyed* townships (e.g., Orange Township, Hancock County, Figure 7a, etc.). In most instances where this is not the case, a combination of surveyed township, range, and section lines delimits the minor civil divisions (e.g., Van Buren Township, Hancock County, Figure 7a, etc.). Other types of survey lines and/or water boundaries, often in combination with township, range, or section lines, bound most of the remaining civil townships in systematically surveyed rural Ohio. A few township lines in this area are parallel to, but not coincident with, surveyed lines, and even fewer are quite unrelated to the survey system. In spite of certain irregularities, there is at the present time a remarkable agreement between minor civil division boundaries and original survey lines in the systematically surveyed parts of Ohio. This situation is exemplified by area S (Figure 21a), which also shows the relationship of properties to civil administrative boundaries. Only slightly more than 1 mile of township line was crossed by a total of 6 individually owned properties in example S in 1955. These figures are approximately the same as for S in 1875, although the locations of straddling properties are not usually the same (Figures 16a and 21a).[15]

In contrast to this high degree of coincidence between administrative and property boundaries in S, nearly all properties peripheral to civil township lines in U straddled these boundaries in 1955 as they had in 1875, in which year only about 3 miles of property lines in that area coincided with civil township lines. The same figures were true of 1955, with the location of coinciding township and property lines essentially the same (Figures 16b and 21b). Elsewhere in the unsystematically surveyed example area, properties straddle civil lines in an indiscriminate manner. Thus in 1955 there was one property unevenly divided among three different counties (and, therefore, three townships), several properties partly in two different counties, and a number in three different townships of the same county. Over a quarter of all properties in example area U in some fashion straddled civil boundaries in 1955.

In rural, agricultural areas today, as at all earlier periods, the

[15]The ease of compiling property maps of the rectangular area as compared with the difficulty of the operation for the Virginia Military District has to be experienced to be appreciated. For example, to arrive at the total amount of land in a property contained partly in four different civil divisions, it is necessary to obtain four plats, which might be of different scales, compare the edges of these, and total at least four (usually odd-fractioned) figures. If, in addition to being contained in more than one civil division, Virginia Military District original survey boundaries extend through the property (rather than the property being contained in one such unit), the number of figures to be totaled to find the size of a modest-sized property might run as high as ten. In view of this, it is not surprising that the basic work sheets for the maps of area U took over four times as long to compile a those for S.

greater share of all local tax is derived from real estate.[16] Taxation districts in rural areas are generally the minor civil divisions, and this characteristic is true also of the example areas. It can make a great deal of difference on which side of a taxation boundary one's property happens to be situated. Even in different townships of the same county it is possible to pay one-third more in local taxes in some minor civil divisions than in others.[17] The difficulty of assessing the mill tax on land in areas where a property may be partly in two or more districts can be imagined, especially since the properties are often composed of imperfectly surveyed and recorded, odd-shaped, odd-fractioned parcels of land. To add to the problem, county surveyors do not always know precisely the location of the civil division boundaries for which they are responsible in the Virginia Military District.[18] To solve these problems, which affect the people occupying the land in the most vital ways, some county treasurers (the elected officials responsible for these matters) will come to an agreement among themselves to "exchange" overlapping areas at the taxation district lines in an effort to reach some equitable solution.[19] This is done partly to overcome objections of landowners to paying taxes to two (or more) counties. The comparative simplicity of property tax assessment in the rectangularly surveyed areas, where almost all properties are neatly contained within the township and county and where, in addition, the parcels of land are easily measurable, their areas often being in even numbers of acres, can be appreciated.[20]

---

[16]Rose, *op. cit.*, p. 149.

[17]This is the case in the counties concerned where the tax levies for selected years were examined. In Madison County in 1958, for example, the tax rate per thousand dollars of valuation varied from $19.30 in Darby Township to $30.20 in adjacent Pike Township, both of which fall in example area U. From the printed form, 1958 Tax Levies, Madison County, Ohio, enclosed with tax bills for that year.

[18]Several county officials, surveyors, and engineers in different parts of the District complained of this problem. It appears that although monuments or stone markers may be set up in the fields, farmers are apt to remove them if they interfere with agricultural operations.

[19]Information obtained through interviews with the local officials involved.

[20]Francis J. Marschner, *Boundaries and Records in the Territory of Early Settlement from Canada to Florida with Historical Notes on the Cadaster and its Potential Value in the Area,* United States Department of Agriculture, Washington, D.C., 1960, pp. 59-60. This study is, in part, a plea for improvement of the cadaster in unsyste-

SCHOOL DISTRICTS

Another administrative division which vitally affects the life of communities is the school district. Like county and township boundaries, school district boundaries have undergone important changes over the years. Provisions for education in Ohio began before substantial white settlement. The Ordinance of 1785, as previously indicated, provided that section 16, or ¹⁄₃₆th of every township, would be reserved for sale for the maintenance of public schools within the township.[21] In the case of the Virginia Military District school land, an amount equivalent to ¹⁄₃₆th of the tract lay beyond the boundaries of the District. In all, over 700,000 acres of land were set aside to raise revenue for educational purposes in Ohio.[22]

At first, education in rural Ohio was purely a local responsibility. The township trustees were empowered to divide the townships into school districts, to levy a local tax for the construction of schoolhouses in the township, and to utilize the monies arising from the sale of school lands. By 1837 there were about 8,000 school districts in the 1,129 civil townships into which Ohio was then subdivided, giving an average of approximately 7 school districts per township; actually the number varied from 2 to 18.[23] In spite of greatly increased population in the state, there are now only about one-third of the number of school districts which existed in Ohio a century ago. This reduction has resulted from the consolidation of schools permitted by improved transportation facilities.[24] However, consolidation has

---

matically surveyed areas; the author recommends for this purpose the use of controlled vertical air photographs with suitable annotation. Sir Bernard O. Binns in his *Cadastral Surveys and Records of Rights in Land,* United Nations, 1953, pp. 1-66, expresses the opinion that air survey has not superseded ground survey for cadastral purposes.

[21]*Journals of the American Congress,* Washington, D.C., 1823, Vol. 4, p. 521.

[22]George W. Knight, "History of Educational Progress in Ohio," in *Historical Collections of Ohio* (2 vols.), Henry Howe (Editor), Columbus, 1902, Vol. 1, p. 138.

[23]Edward A. Miller, "History of the Educational Legislation in Ohio from 1803 to 1850," *Ohio Archaeological and Historical Publications,* Vol. 27, 1919, p. 29, and Aumann and Walker, *op. cit.,* pp. 222-244.

[24]The landscape of rural Ohio today is dotted with one-room schoolhouses which served, or in some cases still serve, the local school districts (see photograph, Figure 37a). Some of these substantial brick buildings now function as churches, township and grange halls, dwellings, stores, gas filling stations, barns, and even

progressed unevenly over the state. Control and financing of the schools has passed from township authorities to municipal, county, and state officials.

It was considered necessary, in order to gain a proper overview of the situation, to study more than just the example areas; a map resulting from this study, which embraces practically all of examples S and U, covering a four-county region and containing school districts of the four major types, is included as Appendix G.[25] However, the detailed relationship between property lines, school districts, and original survey boundaries cannot properly be shown on a map of that scale. Therefore, an even more detailed map of the example areas which would bring out these factors was prepared (Figure 22).[26] Careful inspection of this map will reveal that school districts in the example areas are not confined within the limits of the civil township or even the county. There were 48 miles of school district boundaries in U and 34 miles in S, *c.* 1955. Much more correspondence between civil division and school district lines is evident in area U than in S: 30 miles or 63 per cent of school district boundaries in U, against 11 miles or 32 per cent of school district boundaries in S. Because there is a large degree of correspondence between civil division lines and school district boundaries in U, it follows from the previous discussion that there is little correspondence between school district and property boundaries in this example area. Out of the 48 miles of school district boundaries, about 16 miles, or 33 per cent of these lines, coincide with property lines in U

---

pigsties. Gale W. Baldwin, retired County School Superintendent of Union County, compiled a map of schoolhouses and sites of former schoolhouses of Union County, using county atlases and other sources of information. There were at one time 140 schoolhouses in this modest-sized area against 9 public schools in 1957. Mr. Baldwin did not attempt the almost impossible task of reconstructing the changing school district boundaries of the county. Usually the records of a school district are destroyed when consolidation takes place.

[25]No general map of the school districts in Ohio exists. To keep such a map up to date would require the full-time services of two draftsmen, according to Dr. Robert L. Rohe, Director of School Finance for Ohio, so rapidly are these boundary changes taking place. Many modern school boundaries are established with convenience in bus routing as a primary consideration.

[26]Local school superintendents generally have a manuscript map of the educational districts for which they are responsible in their offices, and it was from such documents that information on Figures 22a and b and on the map, Appendix G, was derived.

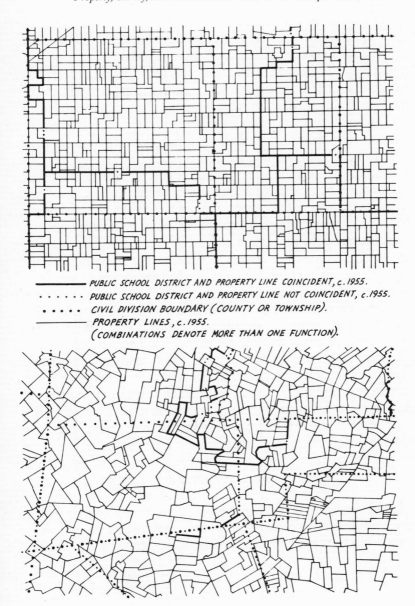

Figures 22a and 22b Relationship of Public School District, Civil, and Property Boundaries, *c.* 1955.

(Figure 22b). The situation with respect to these two sets of lines in systematically surveyed example area S is not a simple reversal of the above. Although there is little coincidence of civil and school district lines in S, there is a great degree of correspondence between school district and property lines in this area; less than 2 miles (6 per cent) of the 34 miles of school district boundaries were *not* coincident with property lines in 1955. A comparison of the maps, Figure 22 and Appendix G, will help clarify these complex relationships.

At the local level much attention is paid to school district boundaries by parents of school-age children as well as by school officials, so it is important that they be well defined.[27] When a property is severed by a school district line, the children of the landowner go to the schools of the school district in which the dwelling is located, unless a special plea is entered and approved. As previously pointed out, the situation with respect to school districts in Ohio, as elsewhere in the nation, is extremely fluid because of a transportation revolution. Some aspects of this will be dealt with in a subsequent chapter in which the connection between roads and survey divisions will be treated.

Insofar as the modern rural school district is no longer contained within the limits of a civil township or county, it is less a creature of the original surveys (at least in systematically surveyed Ohio) than it was hitherto. In the school as in the conservancy district, mentioned earlier, we can see a breakdown of the hegemony of the civil division.

FIELD AND WOODLOT LINES

The characteristics so far examined are alike in that they are all symbolized on existing maps, either manuscript or published materials. Much of their interrelated nature may not be appre-

[27]School tax rates are uniform throughout the entire school district irrespective of the general rate applying to the taxing district in which they are contained. It is the responsibility of the Auditor of County A to send the correct proportion of tax money to his opposite number in County B in cases where part of the school district of County B extends into County A. The greater part of local tax money is used for educational purposes in the areas discussed in this study. Information supplied by officials of the counties concerned.

ciated because only a limited number of characteristics appear on any particular map; nevertheless they have cartographic expression. Field patterns differ in two important ways from the foregoing. In the first place, maps of field lines are not generally available for the example areas and, second, the accurate reconstruction of field lines over these example areas at a much earlier date is not feasible.

Figures 23a and 23b show field and woodlot boundaries in example areas S and U respectively. These lines were drawn from about 50 overlapping vertical air photographs from the United States Department of Agriculture, Production and Marketing Administration. The scale of the photographs in both cases was 1:20,000; those used for Figure 23a were dated August 1949 and those for Figure 23b, May 1952 (Figures 1a and 1b are small examples of this air photo coverage). All the photographs were of excellent quality, allowing a high degree of accuracy in the interpretation of field boundaries, some of which were checked on the ground. The bare outlines of the boundaries of fields and woodlots in the two example areas, as they would appear from an airplane on a clear day, are laid out for inspection in the two parts of Figure 23.

The swirling mass of lines oriented in all directions and enclosing patches of land of many different shapes and sizes (Figure 23b) might, in their gross form, resemble the field boundaries in portions of Western Europe or many other parts of the unsystematically surveyed areas of the world. Some of the field boundaries of example area U terminate a streams or at transportation lines which, in this area, extend in all directions. Other field and woodlot lines are coextensive with the irregular warrant and property boundaries of the Virginia Military District or are parallel to these lines. Still other field boundaries in the area are convenient subdivisions, unrelated in any particular fashion to other lines.

By contrast, field boundaries in example area S (Figure 23a) show the unmistakable influence of the rectangular survey system. To be sure, some field and woodlot boundaries in this area of systematic subdivision terminate at streams or at transportation lines which do not conform to the grid pattern; some

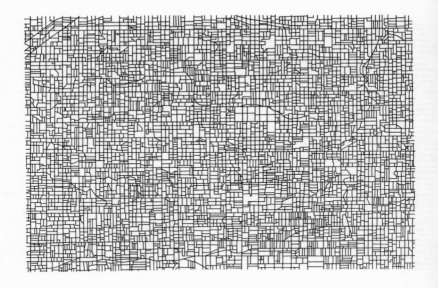

Figures 23a and 23b Field and Woodlot Boundaries in the Example Areas, *c.* 1955.

properties are subdivided into fields by diagonal boundaries. However, these cases are exceptional, and the great majority of field lines and woodlot boundaries are oriented in cardinal directions and enclose rectangular parcels of land.

In general, field boundaries in the systematically surveyed example (Figure 23a) appear to divide the land more finely than do these lines in the unsystematically surveyed area (Figure 23b). Accordingly, we would expect to find many larger fields in U than in S and this is, in fact, the case. Thus about 25 per cent of unsystematically surveyed area U is in fields or woodlots in excess of 40 acres each, the largest field being approximately 120 acres in extent. Only about 1 per cent of the land area in systematically surveyed example area S is subdivided into fields or woodlots larger than 40 acres (1/16 section). The largest field in this example area is approximately 80 acres.

In earlier sections of this work, it has been indicated that transportation lines, especially roads, bear a more or less positive relationship to the system of cadastral survey employed in a particular area, and affect land subdivision at different levels. Thus the location of some of the boundaries in Figures 23a and 23b can only be appreciated in relation to lines of transportation, the subject of the next chapter.

V.

Land Subdivision, Transportation Lines, and Related Features, c. 1875 and c. 1955

PERHAPS THE MOST OBVIOUS difference between the systematic and unsystematic surveys is the nature of the road network developed under these contrasting types of land subdivision. In reasonably level areas, it is possible to discern the boundary between the Virginia Military District and the systematically surveyed parts of the state, even on general Ohio highway maps, by the road pattern alone. On detailed county road maps, where all the public roads are shown, the difference is even more evident. Roads are important to this study for two special reasons. In the first place, roads subdivide as well as unite areas; second, the road network is related, to a greater or lesser degree, to the fundamental survey lines. These two particular aspects of road patterns, of the many that might be examined, will be emphasized in the following discussion. A chapter was devoted to a consideration of survey, administrative, and property units in 1875 in the example areas, and another to these and other divisions in 1955. In this chapter, to afford a closer comparison, a different technique will be employed; the various phenomena discussed will be treated topically at the two dates. Thus in the following section we will be concerned with road density both in 1875 and in 1955.

DENSITY OF PUBLIC ROADS, C. 1875 AND C. 1955

Figure 24 consists of two maps illustrating the road network as developed in example areas U and S by 1875.[1] Even the most cursory inspection of the two maps reveals a striking difference in the road pattern. Roads in U (Figure 24b) extend in all directions and enclose irregular patches of land. In contrast, the great majority of roads in S, in 1875, were oriented in cardinal directions most commonly enclosing rectangular areas (Figure 24a). In an effort to discover what relationship road patterns of the example areas might have to earlier routes, an examination was made of records and maps. Apparently no important Indian trail extended through either of the example areas.[2] Similarly, none of the early military roads, which often followed the routes taken by Indian trails, ran through either area S or U. The much-used military road from Fort McArthur (near present-day Kenton) to Fort Findlay (Findlay) lay to the east of example area S; the National Road, an important emigrant trail, was about 10 miles south of the southern limit of U.[3] Apparently the roads in the two example areas were developed by early settlers without benefit or influence of significant pre-existing routeways. The first roads were built through the enterprise of individual pioneers and often bore the names of those who petitioned for their

---

[1] This information is taken from the county atlases described earlier. Usually no distinction is made in these atlases respecting the quality of roads, although occasionally the fact is noted that a road is surfaced with gravel. The great majority of roads in the example areas, in 1875, were dirt roads (though some were plank roads) and were built and maintained locally.

[2] William C. Mills, *Archaeological Atlas of Ohio,* Ohio State Archaeological and Historical Society, Columbus, 1914. The map of Indian trails and villages (p. ix) shows no route through either area U or area S. One Indian enclosure and one mound have been discovered in area S, and one mound in U. However, the density of such sites is much lower in the vicinity of the examples, S and U, than in areas to the south and east in Ohio.

[3] Thomas Donaldson, *The Public Domain,* Washington, D.C., 1884, p. 257. This road, which passed through the center of what is now Madison County, was constructed for the purpose of opening up western lands for settlement from the Atlantic coast. It was funded through the Enabling Act of April 30, 1802, by which 5 per cent (reduced to 3 per cent in the following year) of the net proceeds of the sale of land was applied to developing such routes.

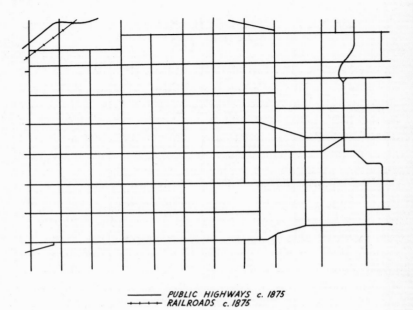

——— PUBLIC HIGHWAYS c. 1875
+—+—+ RAILROADS c. 1875

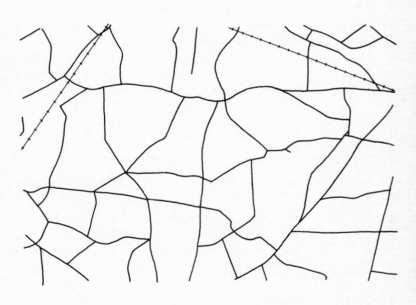

Figures 24a and 24b Public Highways and Railroads in the Example Areas, *c.* 1875.

construction.[4] Land was frequently donated for this purpose, and although a road meant that the farmer lost some land and had to erect and repair more fences, he was usually willing to do this for the obvious transportational advantages.

It is abundantly evident from examination of the two maps of Figure 24 that the road network was much denser (i.e., there were more roads per unit area) in the systematically than in the unsystematically surveyed area in 1875. At this date in U (Figure 24b) there were 125 miles of public roads while in S there were 200 miles of such roads (Figure 24a). In other sample units from the Virginia Military District and from the systematically surveyed parts of rural Ohio, road density figures have been found to be in approximately the same proportion as in example areas U and S. Even where rural population figures are higher, road density is commonly lower in the Virginia Military District than in other parts of Ohio. The fact that there was about 60 per cent more total mileage of public roads in S than in U in 1875 suggests proportional economy in road construction and maintenance in U. At a period when these duties were performed largely through local effort, the inhabitants were affected in a very important respect — the manual labor of the individual or his representatives.[5] In addition to economy in road construction and maintenance in U, less land was used for roads in this area in 1875 than in S. Assuming roads 4 rods wide in both U and S, there would be approximately an additional square mile

[4]The practice, through the years, has been to rename these roads to indicate the settlements they serve. Thus Morgridge Road in Darby Township, Madison County, is now known as Rosedale-Plain City Road. No provision was made for road easements in the United States Land Survey, but at first settlers were usually willing to release land for this purpose because of the advantages of proximity to a highway. Taxes are usually paid on such land, the center of the road serving as the limit where roads separate properties. When a road is abandoned, the land reverts to the properties from which it was originally derived.

[5]"Every able-bodied citizen of twenty-one years or over was obliged by the Act of 1809 to give two days of work each year on the roads of his community. He was privileged to pay a dollar a day or hire a substitute in lieu of such service." (*The History of the State of Ohio*, Carl Wittke (Editor), Vol. 2: *The Frontier State, 1803-1825*, by William T. Utter, Ohio State Archaeological and Historical Society, Columbus, 1942, p. 206.) Among the general historical writings on the state, Chapters 5 and 8 of the volume cited have special applicability to this study. See also Florien Giauque, *The Laws Relating to Roads and Ditches, Bridges, and Water Courses in the State of Ohio*, Cincinnati, 1886, pp. 116-120.

Original Survey and Land Subdivision

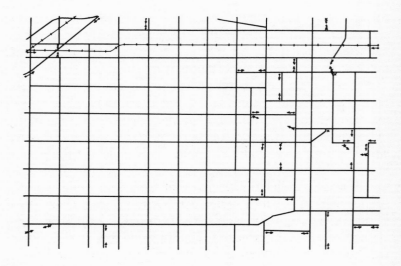

PUBLIC HIGHWAYS c.1955; ═══ HIGHWAYS ADDED 1875 - 1955; ►◄ HIGHWAYS ABANDONED 1875 - 1955)
◄──► RAILROADS c.1955; ═══ RAILROADS ADDED 1875 - 1955.

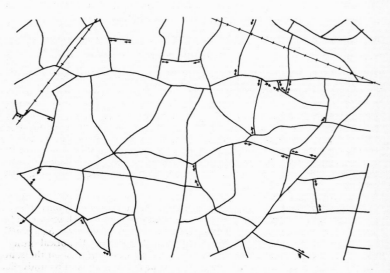

Figures 25a and 25b Public Highways and Railroads in the Example Areas, *c.* 1955.

of land available for purposes other than transportation in U than in S.

The modern public road pattern in the example areas is shown in Figures 25a and 25b.[6] This *arrangement* of highways differs only in detail from the pattern of eighty years earlier, although there was, of course, an enormous improvement in the quality of roads between 1875 and 1955. Public roads of all types in example area U at the later date totaled approximately 145 miles, as against 210 miles in S; there was approximately 45 per cent greater mileage in S than in U, as opposed to 60 per cent more in 1875.

In the unsystematically surveyed area U, approximately 22 miles of new roads were added and 2 miles abandoned in the eighty-year period; in S, 16 miles were added and 6 abandoned. Sites of roads abandoned and constructed between 1875 and 1955 are indicated on Figures 25a and 25b. The difference between the total mileage of roads in U and in S had been reduced over an eighty-year period, but there was still a considerable difference with 65 miles more in the systematically than in the unsystematically surveyed areas. Using the small examples as a basis, one could work out, for large areas, the difference in highway costs — always one of the biggest items in state and local budgets. Figures from the paragraphs above, together with others on the quality of modern roads, are given in Table 3. As will be seen from examination of this table, the mileage of paved roads is about the same in both areas; these figures include not only federal and state paved highways but also paved roads under local authority. Usually only United States and state *paved* highways appear on official and commercial general road maps.

[6]Recent county highway maps of the six counties involved in this study provided the source of information for these maps. Cartographers of the State of Ohio, Department of Highways, were helpful to the writer in explaining their mapping procedures and giving information on the reliability of the maps. There was a possibility of providing a "snapshot" of the road pattern at a period intermediate between 1875 and 1955 from data on maps of the Ohio Cooperative Survey, *c.* 1910. Highway maps based on this excellent source material, the only U.S.G.S. topographic map coverage of the example areas, were constructed but not used in this study. It was felt that changes in the road pattern between 1875 and 1910 were not great enough to justify the inclusion of the maps. In addition, no cadastral maps of a comparable period were available to illustrate the connection between roads and property lines at the later date.

These are the only types of road maps seen by many people, which perhaps explains why the greater density of roads in systematically surveyed areas is not altogether obvious. It is very difficult to estimate road density by ground examination alone without the benefit of detailed maps and air photographs.

An attempt to adjust the road network to the stream pattern accounts for some disturbance in the simple gridiron pattern of roads in the eastern part of S (Figure 25a). It will be noticed that the greatest amount of change in highway location also took place in this area between 1875 and 1955. In general, these changes over an eighty-year period led to a slightly increased degree of rectangularity in the road pattern. The matter of stream/road relationships will be treated subsequently in this chapter.

TABLE 3

MILEAGE OF PUBLIC ROADS, C. 1875 AND C. 1955

Example Area	Total c. 1875	Total c. 1955	Paved c. 1955	Other* c. 1955	Constructed Between 1875 & 1955	Abandoned Between 1875 & 1955
S	200	210	55	155	16	6
U	125	145	56	89	22	2

(All figures rounded)
*In Ohio, other roads according to surface type include those of five lower classes, viz. (in descending order): bituminous-surfaced road (low); metal-surfaced road; soil-surfaced road; graded and drained earth road; unimproved road. (From the official General Highway Maps of the counties concerned and *Classification by Surface Type of Existing Mileage in each County on State Highway, County and Township Systems,* Ohio Department of Highways, Columbus, 1956.)

SURVEY LINES AND PUBLIC ROADS, C. 1875 AND C. 1955

The extent to which public roads are directly related to the original surveys can readily be ascertained by finding the amount of correspondence between fundamental survey lines and highways. In the systematically surveyed area S, approximately 155 miles of roads coincided with section lines in 1875. Since there are 195 miles of section lines, about an 80 per cent positive correspondence existed between fundamental survey lines and roads in the systematically surveyed example area at that time (Figure 26a). At the same period, as previously noted, there were 200 miles of roads in S, so that the percentage of all public roads following section lines was approximately 77 per cent.[7]

In contrast to this, roads usually did not coincide with fundamental survey lines in U in 1875 (Figure 26b). At that date only 22 miles of roads coincided with Virginia Military District original, numbered survey unit boundaries in this example area, out of a total of 270 miles of such lines (approximately 8 per cent). Expressed in another way, 22 miles of roads out of a total of 125, or about 18 per cent of all public roads in U, coincided with fundamental survey lines in 1875. If we consider relationship, direct and indirect, about 180 of the 200 miles (90 per cent) of public highways in the rectangularly surveyed example S extended in the same cardinal directions (E-W, N-S) as the fundamental survey lines in 1875,[8] whereas in U we note little direct and essentially no indirect control.

[7]This high degree of correspondence between public highways and section lines is by no means unusual in fairly level portions of the systematically surveyed areas of the United States. When preparing the contemporary official highway map for the State of Iowa, the writer had to examine all of the 99 county highway maps of that state. Although no measurement was made of the coincidence of section lines and roads in this large area, it was estimated that about 90 per cent of all public highways in Iowa extend along fundamental survey lines.

[8]"In some states all section lines are declared by statute to be public roads, but the landowners are protected in their constitutional right to damages, and it is held that the effect of the statute is to locate roads along the section lines to be opened in the discretion of the county commissioners when the public good requires, and that they cannot be opened without notice and an appraisement of damages. But it is held, under the act of congress granting the right of way for the construction of highways over public lands not reserved for public use, and an act of a territory declaring all section lines public roads, that persons filing on public lands take the same subject to the right of way along section lines for highways and are not entitled to compensation. In such cases it is held that where the road has been established along a controverted line, it follows the true section line wherever that is finally determined. But where no such statute exists there is no presumption that an ordinary road followed a section line throughout its course merely because it is shown to have followed it for a portion of the course." (Byron K. Elliot and William F. Elliot, *The Laws of Roads and Streets,* 4th ed., Vol. 1, pp. 501-502.) In conversation with the writer, Charles Y. Williams, Attorney, Examiner of the Ohio State Department of Highways, indicated that there is not, and has never been, a statute declaring section lines to be public roads in Ohio. Compensation is awarded for easements including road widening in Ohio today. One person knowledgeable on such matters opined: " . . . there is often a lawsuit, but the state generally gets what it needs."

Original Survey and Land Subdivision

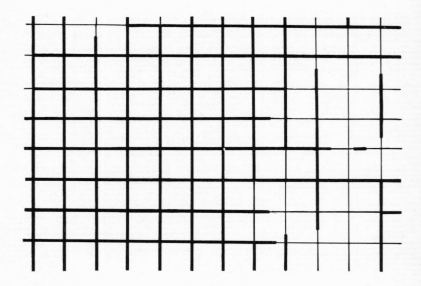

PUBLIC HIGHWAY AND FUNDAMENTAL SURVEY LINE
(SECTION, ABOVE ; V. M. D UNIT, BELOW) COINCIDENT, c. 1875.

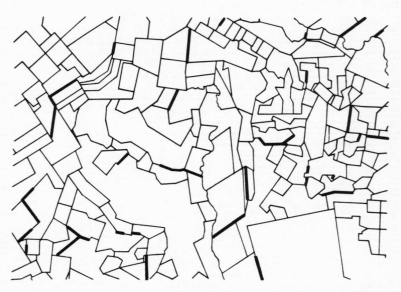

Figures 26a and 26b Relationship of Public Highways and Fundamental Survey Lines in the Example Areas, *c.* 1875.

In the eighty years that elapsed between 1875 and 1955, the situation with respect to the coincidence of roads and fundamental survey lines did not change radically in the two example areas (Figures 27a and 27b). Out of a total of 210 miles of public roads in example area S, at the later date, 162 miles coincided with section lines. Thus 77 per cent of all roads followed section lines, the same percentage of coincidence that existed in 1875. Since the mileage of section lines always remains the same and there were, in 1955, more roads along section lines (7 out of the 10 miles added), the percentage of coincidence between fundamental survey lines and roads has, naturally, increased. Approximately 83 per cent of section lines were the location of roads, against 80 per cent in 1875. As will be illustrated later, the major reason that some section lines in area S have not served as the sites of roads is the particular location of streams, though in many areas the lines of transportation extend without reference to water features.

In area U between 1875 and 1955 there was a net addition of about 3 miles of public highway taken up along original, numbered survey unit boundaries, and 17 miles not so located. Out of a total of 145 miles of public roads in U, *c.* 1955, approximately 25 miles coincided with the limits of these fundamental Virginia Military District survey plots. This is rather more than a 17 per cent correspondence of *all* roads with fundamental survey lines, a figure very close to the 18 per cent of eighty years before. Again, because a greater length of highway was constructed along fundamental survey lines than was abandoned along these lines between the two dates, a slightly higher percentage of fundamental survey lines and roads coincided at the later than at the earlier date: 9 per cent in 1955, against roughly 8 per cent in 1875. Figures showing the coincidence of fundamental survey lines and roads in 1875 and 1955 are expressed in Table 4.

A factor of importance in considering the detailed placement of highways in examples S and U is the stream pattern. In these two level areas, physical features other than stream courses apparently played only a minor role in the location of highways. Figure 28 illustrates the network of public roads, the stream

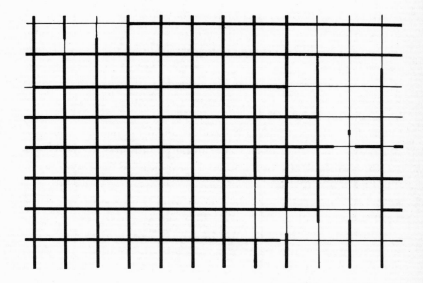

PUBLIC HIGHWAY AND FUNDAMENTAL SURVEY LINE
(*SECTION, ABOVE ; V.M.D. UNIT, BELOW*) COINCIDENT, c.1955.

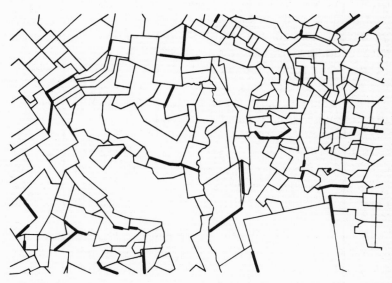

Figures 27a and 27b Relationship of Public Highways and Fundamental Survey Lines in the Example Areas, *c.* 1955.

TABLE 4

COINCIDENCE OF FUNDAMENTAL SURVEY LINES AND PUBLIC ROADS, C. 1875 AND C. 1955

Example Area	Date	Total Mileage of Fundamental Survey Lines	Total Mileage of All Public Roads	Coincidence of Fundamental Survey Lines and Public Roads	Percentage of All Public Roads Coinciding with Fundamental Survey Lines	Percentage of All Fundamental Survey Lines Coinciding with Public Roads
S	1875	195	200	155	77	80
U	1875	270	125	22	18	8
S	1955	195	210	162	77	83
U	1955	270	145	25	17	9

(All figures rounded)

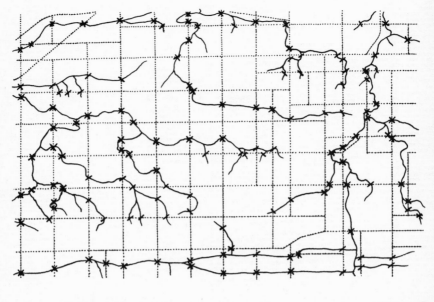

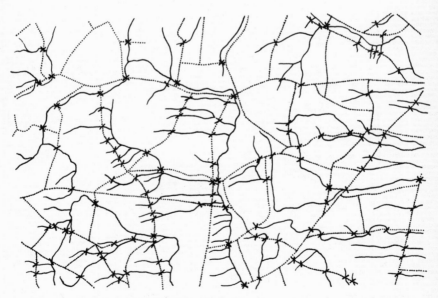

Figures 28a and 28b Relationship of Roads, Streams, Bridges, and
Culverts in the Example Areas, *c.* 1955.

pattern, and road/stream crossings of all types in both example areas, *c.* 1955.[9]

Public highways are usually placed in such a manner as to reduce to a minimum road/stream crossings at the *wider* parts of streams in area U; in S, roads frequently angle across even the narrow part of a stream in such a fashion that a large bridge is required. The pioneers who blazed the trails that were later developed into public highways in the unsystematically surveyed area knew the land well and avoided, as far as possible, the principal stream courses which, as in S, form the most significant terrain obstacles in the area. In example area U there are 150 miles of streams, and *c.* 1955 there were 121 bridges of all kinds (Figure 28b). However, because of the particular placement of roads with respect to streams, 97 of these bridges are minor structures (highway culverts of less than 20-foot span), and 24 are general highway bridges.[10] These two types of road/stream crossings are shown by different symbols on Figure 28.

In the systematically surveyed example area S (Figure 28a) in 1955 there were 110 miles of streams of all kinds and 134 road/stream crossings. Because there is more mileage of public roads and public roads plus streams in S than in U, the fact that in S a somewhat smaller total of streams requires a greater *number* of bridges is no particular surprise. However, the character of the bridges, more than their somewhat greater number, represents an important difference between the two areas. In S, 81 out of the 134 bridges (over 60 per cent) were general highway bridges of 20-foot span or over, and 53 were highway culverts (usually a metal or concrete pipe with earth piled over it). We have seen that a few miles of section lines in S are not

[9]Until the period of modern highway improvement, there were few bridges, except foot bridges, in either example area; accordingly, no map is included showing bridges *c.* 1875. Prior to the World War I era, most streams had to be forded, although a few older bridges are to be found in the example areas today. An illustration of a covered bridge in U appears in Figure 38b.

[10]Information on bridges in the area was taken from the county highway maps of the counties concerned. Officials of the Bureau of Bridges, Ohio State Department of Highways, were most helpful in answering the writer's questions respecting the nature and quality of bridging in the two example areas, and in general. If the road pattern of S in 1955 is superimposed over area U, the number of road/stream crossings is 155, whereas if the U road pattern is placed over area S the number is 90.

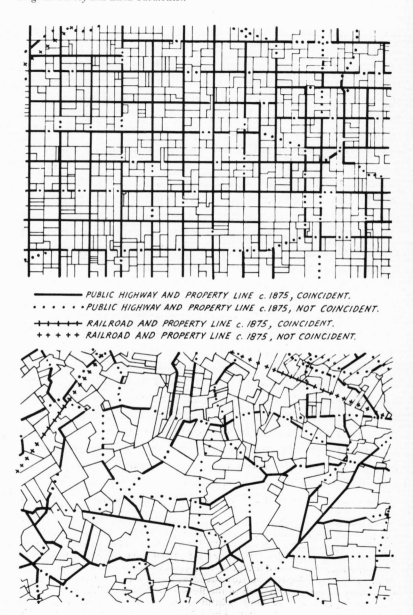

PUBLIC HIGHWAY AND PROPERTY LINE *c.* 1875, COINCIDENT.
••••••PUBLIC HIGHWAY AND PROPERTY LINE *c.* 1875, NOT COINCIDENT.
++++++ RAILROAD AND PROPERTY LINE *c.* 1875, COINCIDENT.
+ + + + + RAILROAD AND PROPERTY LINE *c.* 1875, NOT COINCIDENT.

Figures 29a and 29b Relationship of Transportation Lines and Property Boundaries in the Example Areas, *c.* 1875.

taken up as roads; the major reason for this is an attempt to adjust the highway to the stream pattern. However, in most instances no adjustment is made, so that roads cross streams indiscriminately; hence, the much greater number (and percentage) of larger and costlier bridges in the systematically surveyed area S than in the unsystematically surveyed area U (81 against 24).[11] In a pilot study of other systematically and unsystematically surveyed areas, the writer found that the characteristic referred to above was present to approximately the same degree in the respective sample areas as in S and U.[12]

Important as this matter of the relationship between fundamental survey lines and roads might be in explaining the particular spatial arrangement of certain phenomena, the correspondence or lack of correspondence between property boundaries and roads is perhaps more intimately connected with the everyday lives of people occupying the land.

PROPERTY BOUNDARIES AND TRANSPORTATION LINES, C. 1875 AND C. 1955

The two maps of Figure 29 illustrate the relationship between property lines and roads in the example areas *c.* 1875. At this period, in unsystematically surveyed area U, approximately 55 out of a total of 125 miles of roads *severed* individual properties. The remaining 70 miles of roads coincided with property lines; expressed otherwise, 56 per cent of road mileage separated different properties and 44 per cent cut through (or severed) individual holdings (Figure 29b). Of the 10 miles of railroads in area U, 7 miles cut through properties in 1875.

In systematically surveyed area S, about 35 miles of roads

---

[11]Files on the cost of bridges at the Ohio State Department of Highways were made available to the writer, but officials of the Bureau of Bridges warned of the difficulty of using this source of information. When these records were examined, it was found that some bridges in the example areas were too old to be listed and others were built when the cost was only a fraction of today's price.

[12]Along one mile of section line in a rural area near example area S, the writer found six large bridges. This is the case because a considerable stream meanders back and forth across a fundamental survey line, now the location of a highway. There would be only one large bridge, probably, in a similar situation in an unsystematically surveyed area.

severed individual properties in 1875 and 165 miles of roads out of a total of 200 (82 per cent) coincided with property lines. Thus only about 18 per cent of road mileage cut through holdings in S in 1875, as against 44 per cent in U. As examination of Figure 29a will reveal, almost all roads not oriented in cardinal directions in S cut through properties, accounting for the greater share of severance in this area, *c.* 1875. The railroad in S at this date, which extended diagonally across the cardinal lines, also severed properties throughout the 2 miles of its length.[13]

Severance of property by roads may have both advantages and disadvantages to the rural dweller. For example, if a public road cuts through a property in an advantageous fashion, it may serve as an access road for the farm itself. On the other hand, roads frequently fragment properties into awkward-shaped, uneconomic parcels of land. Where roads (or railroads) must be crossed by animals going from pasture to pasture, other problems arise. Less pedestrian, but not less significant, are the legal implications of the cutting through of holdings by lines of

[13]The first railroad tracks in any part of the two example areas were laid down in S in 1853. The last railroad to be added in these areas was also in S in 1882; note how this railroad, shown on Figure 30a (but not on Figure 29a), follows a half-section line through most of its course and a quarter-section line through most of the remainder. The railroads in U were constructed between the two dates above, and the following quotation affects that area. It is part of a deed copied from manuscript records contained in the "Railroad Book" in Union County Courthouse and gives details of the transfer of land from individuals to a railroad company: "A. A. Woodworth and Wife to C. C. & C. Rail Road, know all men by these presents that we A. A. Woodworth and Hilah Woodworth wife of said A. A. Woodworth the grantors in consideration of the sum of four hundred dollars in hand paid by the Cleaveland [*sic*], Columbus and Cincinnati Rail Road Company the grantees do give, grant, bargain, sell and convey unto the said grantees, their successors and assignees the following described premises situated in the State of Ohio in the County of Union and in Military Survey, No. 7789 and bounded as follows: Beginning at a stake in the northerly line of H. Gillespie's land and southerly line of said Woodworth's land, S 42° E, two poles and one foot from the center of the travelled track of the Rail Road now owned by said Company thence parallel with said Rail Road now owned by said Rail Road and two poles and one foot from the center of the track as now travelled N 33 1/4° E, 310 poles to a stake in the northerly line of said Woodworth land . . . etc., etc." This document was dated 1869. Eight acres of land were involved in this transfer; note the reference to a Military Survey number in this description. On the maps of the present study, railroads are represented by a single, straight line (crossed) because, at the scale used, it is not feasible in another way to express such a narrow swath (in the above case, 68 feet).

transportation, in particular, compensation for severance of properties when easements for new highways are made. The contemporary situation with respect to severance of land by roads in areas S and U is discussed below.

The two pairs of maps, Figures 29a and 30a, 29b and 30b, illustrate that in both example area S and example area U there was emphatically less severance of properties by roads in 1955 than in 1875. In the rearrangement of property boundaries and change of title over an eighty-year period, a strong tendency in the direction of coincidence of property lines and roads is evident.[14] The extent to which this is true for the example areas is shown by the following figures. In the unsystematically surveyed example U, 37 miles of roads out of a total of 145 miles severed properties in 1955, or 26 per cent against 44 per cent in 1875; in the systematically surveyed example S, only 10 per cent of road mileage now cuts through properties (22 out of a total of 210 miles) as opposed to 18 per cent eighty years ago. Along the few miles of railroad tracks in both areas we note the strong tendency for properties to terminate at these rights of way in both example areas, but it has progressed further in S than in U. Thus there are now 14 miles of railroads in systematically surveyed example S, only 2 miles of which sever properties; in the unsystematically surveyed example U, 4 out of a total of 10 miles of railroad tracks now (*c.* 1955) cut through properties. Detailed study of the two pairs of maps will reveal the precise arrangement of transportation and property lines at the two dates, illustrate the local situation with respect to severance along new highways, and show the relationship of railroads to section lines. Table 5 brings together figures which are discussed in the preceding paragraphs.

PROXIMITY AND ACCESSIBILITY, C. 1875 AND C. 1955

Attention has already been given to the matter of road density in example areas S and U in a previous section of this chapter.

[14]When land is sold and estates are divided, often the division is made along roads. There are good reasons for this, being related particularly to the increased use of farm machinery, which often makes uneconomical the cultivation of a small, odd-shaped, severed plot of land.

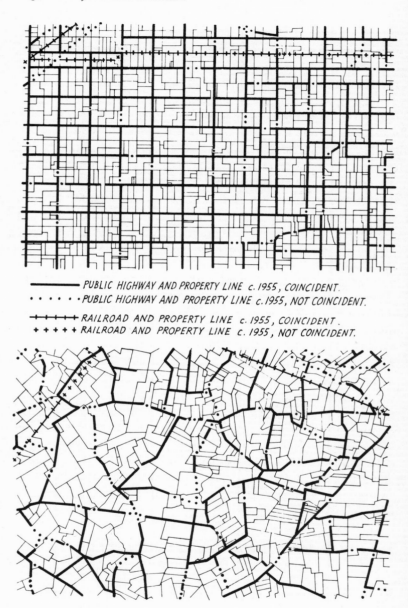

PUBLIC HIGHWAY AND PROPERTY LINE c. 1955, COINCIDENT.
• • • • • • PUBLIC HIGHWAY AND PROPERTY LINE c. 1955, NOT COINCIDENT.

┼┼┼┼┼ RAILROAD AND PROPERTY LINE c. 1955, COINCIDENT.
+ + + + + RAILROAD AND PROPERTY LINE c. 1955, NOT COINCIDENT.

Figures 30a and 30b Relationship of Transportation Lines and Property Boundaries in the Example Areas, *c.* 1955.

There it was demonstrated that in 1875, as in 1955, emphatically less mileage of public roads existed in the unsystematically surveyed area than in the systematically surveyed one. This difference in the density of roads per unit area, as well as in the particular spatial arrangement of the road network in the respective examples, is, naturally, not without its effect on the degree of accessibility within area S and area U. One of the indicators of this characteristic is the amount of land of a given distance or more from a public highway, another the size of road-bounded plots of land. In an effort to discover the degree of accessibility or, perhaps more precisely, proximity to roads in the example areas, the amount of land half a mile or more from a public highway was measured. The figure of half a mile was chosen because if all section lines were taken up as roads, there would be no point more than this distance from a highway in the systematically surveyed area.

TABLE 5

SEVERANCE OF PROPERTIES BY LINES OF TRANSPORTATION,
C. 1875 AND C. 1955

| Example Area | Date | Total Mileage | | Severance of Properties | | | |
| | | Public Roads | Railroads | Public Roads | | Railroads | |
				Miles	Per cent	Miles	Per cent
S	1875	200	2	35	18	2	100
U	1875	125	10	55	44	7	70
S	1955	210	14	22	10	2	14
U	1955	145	10	37	26	4	40

(All figures rounded)

The patches of black in the two parts of Figure 31 show the location of plots of land half a mile or more from a public road in the respective example areas in 1875. In the preparation of these maps and the following pair, cognizance was taken of the roads peripheral to as well as within the areas. But, as shown on Figures 31a and 31b, only that portion of the road-bounded areas occurring in the 100-square-mile example areas is mapped.

Eighty years ago, approximately 18 square miles, or 18 per cent, of the unsystematically surveyed example area U were half a mile or more from a public road (Figure 31b). At the same

BLACK PATCHES = LAND ½ A MILE OR MORE FROM A PUBLIC HIGHWAY c. 1875

Figures 31a and 31b Land Half a Mile or More from a Public Highway
in the Example Areas, c. 1875.

period, *c.* 1875, only about 1.5 square miles (1.5 per cent of the area) were half a mile or more from a public highway in S (Figure 31a). The great degree of proximity in almost all parts of S was due to the greater mileage of roads and to the particular geometrical arrangement of these roads, which in this example area, for the greater part, is directly related to the original subdivision of the land.[15] Like some other factors considered in this study, the distance from public roads has both negative and positive aspects. Some of man's activities are better carried on in large areas uninterrupted by roads, others where there is a maximum of accessibility.

Changes in the proximity of land to roads wrought by the minor changes in the arrangement of highways in the two example areas over an eighty-year period, are illustrated by Figures 32a and 32b. In the unsystematically surveyed area in 1955, 13 square miles (13 per cent of the total area of U) were half a mile or more from a public highway. Approximately one-third of a square mile, only 0.3 per cent of example area S, was distant by half a mile or more from a public road in 1955. Public roads newly constructed in both areas between 1875 and 1955 were placed in such a manner as to reduce substantially the amount of land half a mile or more from public highways. At the end of this eighty-year period, however, there was still a great deal more land closer to roads in S than in U.[16]

---

[15]Other important aspects of the geometry of road patterns will occur to the reader; for example, the automobile accident rate in the systematically surveyed areas, where road junctions are commonly four-way crossings with roads at 90° to each other, in contrast to the accident rate in unsystematically surveyed areas where highway junctions are usually three-way with the roads arranged at no particular angle with respect to each other. This problem is under study by highway safety engineers who, as yet, report no positive conclusions. Other topics more or less related to the matter of original surveys might be investigated, such as the economy of movement in certain directions from point to point, under one arrangement of roads or another. These and other matters were not examined, being regarded as sufficiently removed from the central core of this study to constitute separate investigations. The road offset at a correction line is a commonly remarked-upon phenomenon; however, many people living in systematically surveyed areas do not know the reason for the prevailing rectilinear patterns.

[16]In U, as in other unsystematically surveyed areas examined, it was noted that private driveways to farms, etc., tend to be longer on the average, and therefore greater in aggregate, than in the systematically surveyed localities studied.

BLACK PATCHES ▪ LAND ½ A MILE OR MORE FROM A PUBLIC HIGHWAY c. 1955

Figures 32a and 32b   Land Half a Mile or More from a Public Highway in the Example Areas, *c.* 1955.

Mention has already been made of the fragmentation of land areas by a road network; the plots of land which result from this kind of subdivision are very different in U and in S with respect to both size and shape. The sizes of all road-bounded pieces of land contained wholly or in part in the example areas in 1875 and 1955 are plotted on the graph, Figure 33. As shown by this illustration, the systematically surveyed area S, both in 1875 and in 1955, contained a great many more road-bounded plots than did U. There were 45 such pieces of land, wholly or in part in

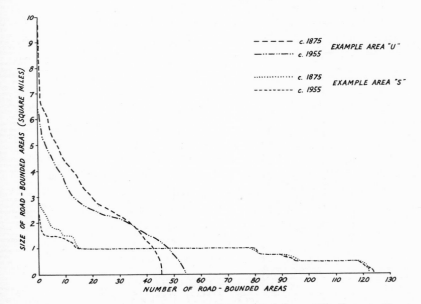

Figure 33 Number and Size of Road-Bounded Areas Wholly or in Part in the Example Areas, *c.* 1875 and *c.* 1955.

unsystematically surveyed area U in 1875, against 122 in S at the same time; thus S had well over twice as many road-bounded parcels of land in 1875 as did area U. In the size of these plots of land, the graph shows as great a difference as in their number in the respective example areas. The pieces of road-bounded land in U, in 1875, as plotted on the graph, form a fairly smooth curve. They range in size from 9.9 square miles to a fraction of a square mile with no particular predominance of any size category. In contrast, over one-half of the road-bounded plots of land in S in 1875 were 1 square mile (sections) and one-fifth were half a square mile each (½ sections); if pieces of land bounded by roads of the sizes 1.5 square miles (1 ½ sections) and .75 square miles (¾ sections) are added to the above, we find that these divisions of the basic unit of the systematic surveys accounted for about 90 per cent of the patches of road-bounded land by number in 1875.

Over three quarters of a century of land use in the two example areas has produced only minor changes in the characteristic discussed above. It is evident, from Figure 33, that these changes are greater in U than in S. There were 10 more road-bounded plots in unsystematically surveyed area U (55 against 45) in 1955 than in 1875, as compared with a net gain of 2 in systematically surveyed area S (124 against 122) between the same dates. The curve formed by plotting the sizes of all road-bounded patches of land in U in 1955 is a subdued version of the graph of the same characteristic, *c.* 1875. Only in detail does the graph of pieces of land bounded by roads in S in 1955 differ from that of eighty years earlier. From previous sections of this chapter we know that this is a consequence of the fact that the road pattern in the systematically surveyed area has undergone very little change in an eighty-year period. Since the time the first roads were laid down along section lines, the rectangular pattern has become more and more firmly fixed.

ROADS AND CIVIL DIVISIONS

The extent to which local authorities are responsible for public highways in certain states is usually not fully appreciated. This is so, in part, because we are accustomed to seeing only general commercial, and state road maps on which a selection of highways appears. Most of the roads shown on such maps are those under federal or state control.

In Figure 34, as in previous maps in this chapter, *all* of the public highways and roads in example areas U and S are delineated. These roads are classified according to whether they are the responsibility of federal or state authorities on the one hand,

Land Subdivision, Transportation Lines, and Related Features, c. 1875 and c. 1955

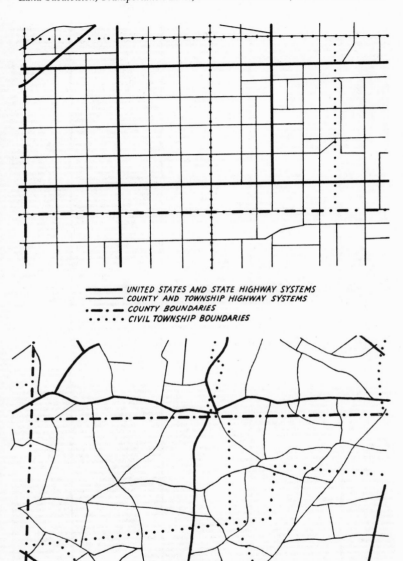

UNITED STATES AND STATE HIGHWAY SYSTEMS
COUNTY AND TOWNSHIP HIGHWAY SYSTEMS
COUNTY BOUNDARIES
CIVIL TOWNSHIP BOUNDARIES

Figures 34a and 34b Road System Designation and Civil Boundaries in the Example Areas, *c.* 1955.

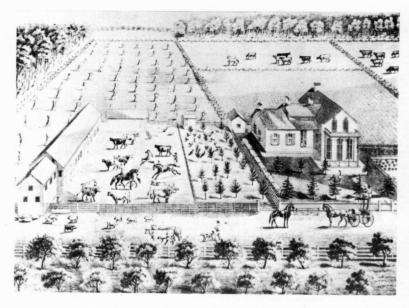

Figure 35a Lithograph illustrating the layout of a farmstead in Northwestern Ohio (from Eberhart's *Atlas of Hancock County, Ohio,* 1875).

Figure 35b Typical scene in the Virginia Military District in the second half of the nineteenth century (from Caldwell's *Atlas of Madison County, Ohio,* 1875). Although of limited artistic merit, such illustrations provide much valuable information on the rural landscape of the period.

Figure 36a   The Scioto River, Marion County, Ohio, a Meeting Place of Systematic and Unsystematic Surveys. A general highway bridge crosses the river.

Figure 36b   Madison County Courthouse, London, Ohio. Late Victorian structures often replaced earlier and more modest courthouses in the counties of the Midwest. The county courthouse is both the symbol and center of county government and the depository of the official records. Local officials have offices in the courthouse, which is usually the tallest and most splendid building in the county.

Figure 37a Abandoned One-Room Schoolhouse, Hancock County, Ohio. Up to a score of such buildings served the educational needs of the rural township in the mid-nineteenth century; the school buildings also functioned as social centers.

Figure 37b Centralized Schoolhouse, Hancock County, Ohio, *c.* 1920. Further consolidation and centralization not only render these buildings obsolete but lead to changes in school district boundaries which, in turn, alter the pattern of rural life.

Figure 38a State Highway Extending N-S Along a Section Line in the Hamlet of Mount Cory, Hancock County, Ohio.

Figure 38b Covered Bridge over Big Darby Creek, Union County, Ohio. Such bridges are now extremely rare in this part of the state.

or of the county and township authorities on the other. As shown on the two maps, Figures 34a and 34b, by all odds the greater mileage of public roads in both example areas was the concern of local authorities in 1955. Of course, these roads do not carry most of the traffic, nor are they usually as well built and maintained as are the federal and state highways. However, they are vitally important to the people occupying the land for reasons already explained and for others which will be obvious to the reader.

In example area U, 37 miles out of a total of 145 miles of public highways in 1955 were maintained by the federal and state governments and 108 miles by local authorities. About 40 miles out of a total of 210 miles of public highways in systematically surveyed example area S at the same time were under federal and state control, and the remaining 170 miles were maintained locally. Thus in 1955 about 81 per cent of all public roads in S were built and maintained locally, and approximately 76 per cent of all public highways in U were so built and maintained.[17] As explained previously, there is much more federal and state control of highways now than at any earlier period.

A great difference exists between example area S and example area U in the manner in which roads are related to the civil division boundaries. As shown on Figure 34b, no coincidence existed in 1955 between either county or civil township boundaries and public roads in the unsystematically surveyed area U. This apparently has always been the case. In contrast, all except 2 miles of the 20 or so miles of county lines in S are marked by roads. Out of approximately 26 miles of civil township boundaries (which are not also county boundaries) in area

---

[17]These percentages compare with those for all public highways in Ohio where, in 1956, out of a total of slightly less than 83,000 miles of roads approximately 16,000 (19%) were under federal or state control, and 67,000 (81%) were administered by county and township authorities. Information on the character of roads and the responsible agency appears in *Classification by Surface Type of Existing Mileage in Each County on State Highway, County and Township Systems,* Ohio Department of Highways, Division of Planning and Programming, Bureau of Planning Survey, 1956.

S, 17 miles were coincident and 9 were not coincident with public roads. This is not unlike the situation in 1875 when all county lines in S, except for 3½ miles, coincided with roads; at the same date, 17 miles out of 26 miles of noncounty, civil township lines were coincident with roads.

The coincidence of roads and civil lines would be a factor of very minor significance if all roads extending along civil lines were federal or state highways. Actually there is only about a one to four chance in Ohio that this will be the case. As shown on Figure 34a, all roads coinciding with civil boundaries in area S in 1955 happened to be locally maintained.

When a locally maintained highway extends along a civil boundary, the responsibility for that road resides jointly with the two civil authorities concerned (either county or township as the case may be). In order to avoid purchasing and operating expensive road-building equipment, some townships relinquish their responsibility for road maintenance, along with appropriate funds, to the county of which they are a part. When a locally maintained highway extends along a county line, the responsibility, with the special problems that this brings, is always shared.[18] If a highway is placed along a civil boundary, there can be little doubt as to the location of that line. In this way, many civil as well as other boundaries in the systematically surveyed area are cemented (or macadamized) on to the surface of the land through highway improvement.

[18]The division is made by agreement between the commissioners (or trustees) of the two civil units concerned. Sometimes the total length of highway involved is divided into two equal distances, sometimes alternate sections are taken and sometimes even a lengthwise division is effected. See Giauque, *op. cit.*, pp. 134-135. Of course, generally, the higher the authority (i.e. federal or state) responsible for the road the better the road, and conversely. However, many roads in Ohio under local control (i.e. county and township) are paved; hence the greater total mileage of roads in this category, in S and in U, than in the category of roads under federal or state control (compare appropriate figures in Table 3 with those in this section).

VI.

Summary and Conclusions

OHIO IS A MEETING PLACE of contrasting methods of land subdivision. In this state are to be found examples of both systematic and unsystematic original cadastral surveys which were conducted under uniform political conditions.

Unsystematic or metes and bounds surveys have been used over most of the settled regions of the earth including the greater part of the area of the original thirteen states of the United States. Under such surveys, boundary lines are arbitrarily selected, while under a systematic method of land subdivision, fundamental survey lines conform to some over-all plan. The rectangular survey system of the United States, which was initiated through the Land Ordinance of 1785, has been lauded as being among the more visionary ideas in the history of mankind. Details of the United States rectangular survey system were worked out as the result of experience of land subdivision in the Old Northwest, the area to which the Land Ordinance and early amendments first applied. The main provisions of this law and subsequent land acts particularly affecting the geography of the United States are: (1) survey prior to settlement, (2) fundamental survey lines oriented in cardinal directions, (3) townships of 6 miles square, (4) sections of 1 square mile, 36 to a township.

Peoples of earlier civilizations, including the Romans, used systematic rectangular surveys. Such methods were also employed in Western Europe in the seventeenth and eighteenth centuries especially but were applied in this area and period only to localities of modest size. Some ideas of systematic surveys took root in the American colonies, and it was partly upon the colonial experience of land subdivision that the legislators drew when framing the famous Land Ordinance of 1785.

In order to understand the reason for the employment in the Ohio country of unsystematic as well as systematic surveys, it is necessary to recall some of the events which led up to the settlement of the Northwest. By reason of her charter, the State of Virginia claimed all of the Ohio territory, a claim contested by other states, especially New York and Connecticut. New York unconditionally relinquished to Congress her claim to western lands in 1780. Following this action, both Virginia and Connecticut relinquished jurisdiction over the Ohio lands, provided that they might retain title to the soil of specified areas. This the Congress of the United States permitted. The area reserved by Virginia to satisfy her generous Revolutionary War land grants is of special concern in this study. It is known as the Virginia Military District of Ohio, contains about one-sixth of the area of that state, and lies between the Scioto and Little Miami rivers.

Nearly all the land of the state of Ohio except the Virginia Military District was originally subdivided for sale and settlement in a systematic manner; Ohio has been regarded as an "experimental" area for the United States National Land System. A number of variations of rectangular land subdivision are to be found in the state. In fact, only the last major tract to be subdivided, Northwestern Ohio, conforms in all respects in its fundamental survey to the National Land System of the United States. Northwestern Ohio has, by some authorities, been considered a model for original surveys in areas of the United States west of this region.

In contrast to the several types of systematic, rectangular land subdivision of most of Ohio is the unsystematic survey used in the Virginia Military District. The size of the fundamental units which applied to this area depended on the rank and length of service of the grantee and varied, in theory, from

15,000 to 100 acres. Such units, however, could be taken up anywhere in the District not yet claimed; they were not necessarily initially surveyed in contiguous plots; nor were there any restrictions as to the boundaries. Furthermore, all of the land in one grant was not required to be in one parcel but could be in separate locations. The result is a patchwork of odd-shaped, various-sized parcels of land with boundaries oriented in any and all directions. A piece of land might be claimed by more than one warrant holder, many plots were not of the acreage prescribed, and some areas were not claimed at all by individuals.

In systematically subdivided parts of Ohio, the surveyed sections are the permanent units used for the description of properties. The original, numbered survey units serve the same function in the Virginia Military District. A great contrast exists between these two sets of units, which are the building blocks of the cadastral surveys in their respective areas. To make feasible the examination of some detailed land characteristics, it was decided to focus upon two areas of 100 square miles each. One of these example areas, U, was taken from the unsystematically surveyed Virginia Military District, and the other, S, from the systematically surveyed area of Northwestern Ohio. These two areas are demonstrably alike in many physical and cultural characteristics (local relief, climate, soil, population, crops, etc.) but are very different in the manner of land subdivision. Through the records kept in the state and various county archives, it is possible to trace the progress of original subdivision in the areas selected for special study. Generally, riparian sites were preferred in the earliest original surveys in U and the interfluves were subdivided later, the whole operation covering a period of several decades. By contrast, all the fundamental subdividing in S occupied only parts of two years, and it progressed in an orderly fashion from east to west.

The principal value of the example areas S and U lies in their representative qualities; hence in this summary their general characteristics are emphasized and the reader is referred to the text for more specific data. Boundary lines of the original, numbered survey plots in unsystematically surveyed example area U extend in all directions and enclose irregularly shaped parcels of land which range in size from approximately 4,000 acres to less than 10 acres. All sections in the systematically surveyed example area are essentially square and contain about 640 acres each. Examination of cadastral maps reveals that only in rare cases do original survey and civil township lines coincide in U, while all civil boundaries are township, range, or section lines in S. In such areas, characteristically, surveyed townships serve as civil townships.

Property boundaries for the example areas, *c.* 1875, were obtained from the county atlases of that period. By 1875 all original claims to land had been made in the Virginia Military District, since four years before this date all lands not reserved were ceded by the federal government to the State of Ohio. Similarly, by 1875, essentially all the land in the systematically surveyed example area was owned and occupied. At this time there was a great difference in both the number and size of properties in the example areas. In U, in 1875, the rather more than 300 contiguous, individually owned properties ranged in size from nearly 2,000 acres to a few acres, with no particular size category predominating. At this same date, in S, there were about two-and-a-third times as many properties as in U, and they ranged in size from 640 acres to a few acres. In addition, most of the properties in S were definite proportions of a section (½, ⅜, ¼, ⅛, 1/16, etc.). In 1875, less than 50 per cent of original survey boundaries in U also functioned as property lines, while over 90 per cent of section lines in S served this purpose at the same date. Properties at the periphery of townships and counties in example area U in 1875 were almost invariably severed by civil boundaries, as were the fundamental survey units to which they are, more or less, related. In contrast, almost all properties terminated at county and civil township lines in S, at the same date, following the situation relative to sections from which they were derived.

From the records of county engineers it is possible to examine the contemporary situation relative to the characteristics discussed above, and this was done for the year 1955. At this date, as at the earlier period, example area U consisted of properties of very unequal size ranging from a 1,300-acre hold-ing to individually owned plots of a few acres. There were about 450 separately owned parcels of land in U in 1955 and approx-imately double this number in S. Properties in S at both the later as well as the earlier date tend to be chiefly in even proportions of the section; they now range in size from 320 acres down to a few acres. Between 1875 and 1955 there was about a 5 per cent decline in original survey boundaries serving as property boun-daries in U (49 per cent to 44 per cent), while there was a slight increase in the percentage of section line mileage in S which delimited properties (91 per cent to 92 per cent) over the eighty-year period. These and other figures suggest greater fluidity in property lines in U than in S and help explain why there has been more litigation concerning property in the Virginia Mil-itary District than in all the remainder of the state combined.

The relationship between civil and property boundaries remained essentially the same in total between the two dates 1875 and 1955, although there were differences in detailed location. In 1875 about one-third, and in 1955 over a quarter of all properties in U straddled civil boundaries in some fashion, individual properties being divided between two, three, or four civil divisions. The fragmentation of these properties by civil lines into awkward-shaped, odd-fractioned parcels of land in the Virginia Military District is a matter of considerable importance. Local land taxes are usually assessed by the township and levied by the county. Therefore, an owner whose property straddles civil divisions has fiscal responsibilities to two or more local authorities. Only a handful of landowners were so affected in 1955 in S, where almost all properties were each contained within a single civil unit as in 1875.

Contemporary manuscript maps of public school districts provided detailed information concerning these important units. In example area U there was, in 1955, a considerable degree of coincidence between civil and school district bounda-ries. It follows, from the foregoing discussion, that in this area there was a lack of coincidence between large portions of the school district boundaries, on the one hand, and original survey and property lines on the other. In S, in 1955, there was less correspondence between civil and school district boundaries than in U. However, in S, almost all school district boundaries are property lines. Since property boundaries in the area are usually parallel to fundamental survey lines, in this manner school district boundaries were related to the basic survey lines in 1955, although less directly than heretofore. Actually, school district boundaries, through consolidation, are changing at such a rate that it is difficult to make meaningful statements about them.

It is virtually impossible to reconstruct field and woodlot boundaries as they existed over the entire example areas, *c.* 1875. Therefore, no comparison was made between these ultimate land subdivisions for S and U at that date. However, from air photographs, maps of the contemporary field and woodlot lines can be made; such maps were produced for this study and the resulting pattern analyzed. The control of the fundamental survey boundaries on the placement of field lines is evident in both areas. In example area U, field boundaries which are oriented in any and all directions enclose fields of very unequal size; a total of about a quarter of the land in the area (*c.* 1955) was in fields which exceed 40 acres each. Fields larger than 40 acres each were very rare in 1955 in S, where about 90 per cent of all field and woodlot lines extended in the same cardinal directions as the fundamental survey lines to which they are related.

The landscape of rural Ohio is both bound together and divided by lines of transportation which are related, in greater or lesser degree, to the original surveys. Examination of the examples U and S and other areas of Ohio revealed that road density (public roads per unit area) was much lower in unsystematically than in systematically surveyed areas, even where population figures are higher. Thus, in 1875, there were approximately 125 miles of public roads in U against 200 miles in S. By 1955 there had been some tendency toward equalization of road mileage in the two areas, but the comparative figures, 145 miles of public roads in U against 210 miles for S, still showed a considerable discrepancy in favor of the latter area. A positive relationship exists between roads and fundamental survey lines in the area of systematic, rectangular subdivision, where about 80 per cent of the section lines functioned as road easements in 1875 and 83 per cent did so in 1955. In this same area, S, close to 80 per cent of all roads followed section lines at both dates. This is in contrast to the situation in U where, in 1875, less than 10 per cent of the fundamental, original survey lines and roads were coincident, and less than 20 per cent of all roads extended along such survey lines. Approximately the same figures apply today in area U. Thus the positive control exercised by fundamental survey boundaries on lines of transportation is very much greater in S than in U at both dates.

The few miles of roads not conforming to section lines in S are often parallel to these boundaries, but are offset some distance to avoid difficult stream crossings. In spite of this modification of the gridiron pattern of roads in S, there are many more large bridges in this area than in U where the roads appear to be much better adjusted to the arrangement of streams. In both example areas the combined mileage of streams of comparable quality and public roads is very nearly the same (more road mileage in S, more miles of streams in U), and in both areas there was not a great difference in the number of bridges (121 in U against 134 in S). But in 1955 there were over three times as many *large* bridges (more than 20-foot span) in S than in U. The reason is that the roads in S, following the section lines, strongly suggest (if not "dictate") where bridges shall be located; bridges in this area usually cut across streams without regard to narrower or wider crossings and even angle across narrow streams. The trailblazers in U were careful to extend roads across large streams only where absolutely necessary.

As indicated, roads characteristically follow section lines in S, which are usually also property boundaries; hence there is little severance of properties by roads in the area. Actually less than 20 per cent of road mileage cut through properties in 1875 in S, and only about half this percentage in 1955. By contrast, nearly 50 per cent of the total road mileage in U in 1875 severed properties and, again, about half of this percentage in 1955. Thus in both areas there is much less severance of properties by roads at the later than the earlier date, but in absolute terms this lack of severance has progressed further in S than in U.

There is a much lower road density in U than in S. Because of this and the particular spatial arrangment of roads in the systematically surveyed area, there is emphatically more land distant from public roads in U than in S. In 1875, close to 20 per cent of all the land in U was distant by half a mile or more from a public road, in comparison with less than 2 per cent for S. Roads added between the earlier and the later date (1875 and 1955) reduced the amount of land distant by half a mile or more from a public road in U to less than 15 per cent. At the latter date only a fraction of 1 per cent of the land in S was distant by more than half a mile from a public road.

Another attribute related to the foregoing is the number and size of road-bounded pieces of land in the example areas. In 1875, the largest road-bounded plot of land in U was almost 10 square miles; the 45 road-bounded plots in this example area ranged in size from nearly 10 square miles down to a fraction of a square mile. At the same date, there were two-and-three-quarter times as many road-bounded parcels of land in S as in U; most of these plots in S were square-mile sections, and most of the remaining plots were even divisions of the section. There were, in 1955, still well over twice as many road-bounded plots in S as in U (55 against 124), showing that in this characteristic there has really been little change over eighty years of settlement. It also illustrates the comparative permanence of basic patterns arising from a particular mode of land subdivision. One result of the larger plots of road-bounded land in U, generally, is that there is a greater total mileage of private roads in the area. In cases of correspondence between roads and survey lines, the latter become, through highway improvement, more and more firmly cemented on to the landscape.

Most of the road mileage of Ohio in both systematically and unsystematically surveyed areas is the concern of local (county and township) authorities. This is an important matter since locally maintained roads which extend along the boundaries of civil divisions are the joint responsibility of the two authorities concerned. In example area U, no problem of this kind exists since no civil boundaries are marked by roads. Most of the mileage of the civil boundaries in S coincide with *locally* maintained public highways and, in this case, no civil administrative boundary is marked by a federal or state highway. Accordingly, responsibility for maintenance of these public roads is shared between the counties and townships involved.

It is evident from this study that the system of original cadastral survey used in a particular area touches the lives of the inhabitants of that locality at many points. A basic cadastral survey, and subsequent land division which proceeds more or less within the framework it provides, affects individuals in other ways not stressed in this study. For example, some persons accustomed to the rectangular method of land subdivision indicate that they experience a sense of disorientation when they go to areas of unsystematic surveys.[1] Conversely, people used to a landscape developed under a metes and bounds survey find the gridiron pattern of the rectangular system, where straight roads stretch out interminably before them, most unappealing. Some of these ideas may be suggested by Figures 35a and 35b, which are illustrations from early county atlases. Figure 35b shows part of a farm complex in the unsystematically surveyed example area. A curving road severs the property of the large landowner whose house is depicted; the whole scene is one of felicitous adjustment between nature and man. The degree to which man is capable of being influenced by, or subjected to, concepts of his own creation is suggested by Figure 35a. This illustration of a property in the systematically surveyed area shows that roads, property, field, and woodlot boundaries conform to the rectangular survey lines. The orientation of the house, barns, and minor structures all follow this plan, and even the ornamental trees appear to be planted in accordance with the rectilinear arrangement of the United States Public Land System. These two

[1]The writer was told of a man who came to Madison County, Ohio, from Illinois with the object of purchasing land. When he encountered, firsthand, an unsystematic survey, he would have nothing to do with it, and bought property farther north in a systematically surveyed locality. Other persons accustomed to the systematic survey indicate that they feel more "secure" in areas where they know directions by the road patterns.

pictures, Figures 35a and 35b, illustrate many elements of the visible landscape in an unsystematic and a systematic survey area, respectively.

This study demonstrates that the effects of a basic system of cadastral survey are of an enduring nature.[2] Modifications of the earlier landscape patterns in the two rural areas of Ohio singled out for detailed examination have occurred during more than a century of settlement. However, these modifications have proceeded within the general framework provided by the original method of land subdivision. There is more fluidity in boundaries and roads in the unsystematically than in the systematically surveyed areas, but in both examples the character of the contemporary geography of occupance and land use owes a great deal to the choice of the original system of land subdivision.[3] Striking differences are evident in the morphology of the cultural landscape developed under these contrasting original survey systems, even though physical conditions are remarkably similar.

The systematic rectangular survey system of the United States served the needs of a nineteenth-century agricultural economy well. It enabled lands newly opened up for settlement to be speedily occupied in a fairly orderly and democratic fashion. But the rectangular pattern has been impressed upon the landscape of the western four-fifths of the United States in a manner scarcely anticipated by the men of Congress who framed the Land Ordinance of 1785. The rectangular system of land subdivision, with its lack of adjustment to the natural landscape, has imposed a straitjacket over large areas where it has been applied, and it is much less suitable for some present-day land uses than for those in practice at the time that it was

[2]Fred Kniffen, "To Know the Land and Its People," *Landscape*, Vol. 9, No. 3, Spring, 1960, p. 23. "The original and traditional modes of dividing land (the French strip layout, the English metes-and-bounds, the system of the American General Land Office) are much slower to change than is the architecture of the houses occupying the land."

[3]"So long as agriculture remained dominant, those first patterns seem to have been retained with a kind of blind tenacity suggesting that usage, rather than economic considerations, was really dominant. It seems to be only when the industrial development calls the big roads into existence that the old rural patterns begin to fall apart." (Personal communication from Professor Vernon Carstensen.)

instituted. There are also obvious drawbacks to the unsystematic surveys, represented in this study by the metes and bounds example of the Virginia Military District of Ohio. Most obvious among these disadvantages is the lack of precision in boundary demarcation, which has led to much litigation and to problems of land tax assessment in the area.

Lessons may be learned from this investigation which may be of use to land settlement and planning agencies. A method of land subdivision which embodies the best features of systematic and metes and bounds surveys would approach the ideal — a cadastral survey sensitive even to subtle variations of the natural landscape but establishing well-defined boundaries.

APPENDIX A

Summary of Major Rectangular Survey Areas in Ohio
(See map, following page)

Name of Area (Numerals Refer to the Map Accompanying Appendix A)	Size of Township Units (Miles Square)	Numbering of Ranges	Numbering of Townships I = Irregular R = Regular	Numbering of Sections (Letters Refer to the Map Accompanying Appendix B)	Orientation (Maximum Deviation from Cardinal Directions)
I — Connecticut Western Reserve	5	XXIV-I W-E	R; 14-1 N-S	(Firelands — F.L. only) C	N 3° W
II — United States Military Tract	5	XX-I W-E	R; 10-1 N-S	X or Y	N 3° E
III — Ohio Company Land	6	XVI-VIII W-E	I; 13-1 N-S	B	N 4° E
IV — Between the Miamis	6	XV-FI* N-S	I; 1-6 W-E	A	N 4° E
Va — Seven Ranges	6	VII-I	I; 20-1 N-S	A	N 3° E
Vb — Congress Lands East of the Scioto	6	XXII-VIII W-E	I; 19-1 N-S	Z	N 4° E
Vc — Congress Lands of Northeastern Ohio	6	XXI-I W-E	I; 25-6 N-S	Z	—
Vd — Congress Lands West of the Miami River	6	I-XIII W-E	I; 15-1 N-S	Z	N 1° W
VI — Northwestern Ohio	6	I-XVII W-E (M = Michigan Survey) IV-I-X	R; 8-1, 1-8 N-S R; 9-10 N-S	Z	—

VII — Virginia Military District-Unsystematically subdivided.

*These ranges are numbered north from the Ohio River; the two partial ranges next to the Ohio River are called Fractional Range No. 1 (FI) and Fractional Range No. 2 (FII). North of FII, ranges are numbered regularly from I in the south to XV in the north.

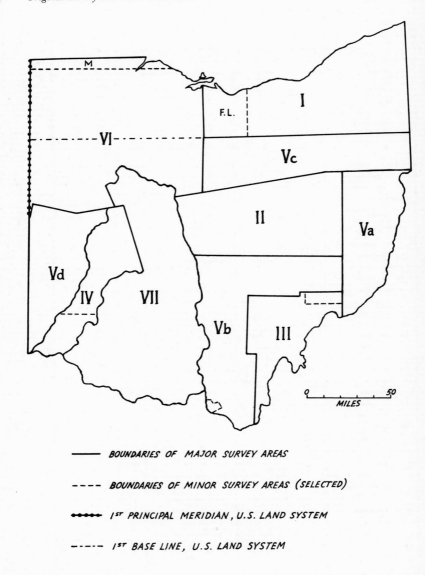

Appendix A   Map of Major Survey Areas or Tracts in Ohio.
(See Table in Appendix A for explanation)

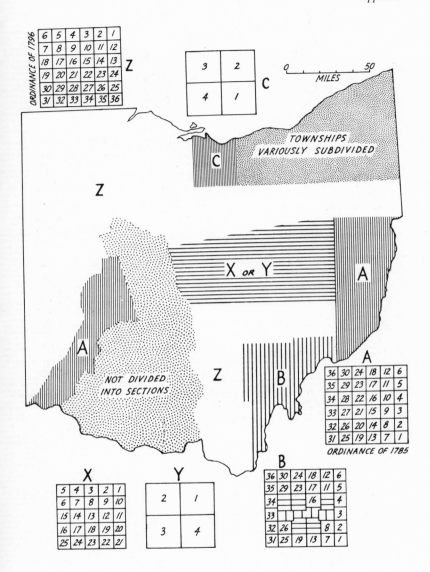

Appendix B   Map of Principal Methods of Numbering Sections in Ohio.

APPENDIX C

POPULATION OF EXAMPLE AREAS IN 1950 AND 1960

	Fraction of Minor Civil Divisions in Example Area	Population 1950	1960
RECTANGULAR			
Hancock County			
Orange Township	All	968	1,008
Van Buren (inc. Jenera)	All	927	905
Madison (exc. Arlington)	40%	266	286
Hardin County			
Liberty Township (exc. Ada)	30%	340	338
Washington	25%	215	216
Small Amounts of Others			
		2,716	2,753
METES AND BOUNDS			
Union County			
Union Township (exc. Milford)	40%	418	426
Darby (inc. Unionville)	40%	575	631
Madison County			
Pike	All	558	506
Canaan	50%	440	519
Darby (exc. Plain City)	50%	280	437
Monroe	36%	222	228
Summerford	12%	101	107
Small Amounts of Others			
		2,594	2,854

Data from: *United States, Census of Population,* PC (1)–37B, Ohio, 1950; 1960; Washington, D.C., 1952, 1961.

APPENDIX D

NATIVITY OF PERSONS RESIDING IN SELECTED
TOWNSHIPS* OF OHIO, 1850†

	SYSTEMATIC *Orange Township* *(Hancock County)*	*UNSYSTEMATIC* *Pike Township* *(Madison County)*
UNITED STATES		
Ohio	504	304
Pennsylvania	110	17
New York	17	12
Maryland	17	2
Connecticut	1	6
New Jersey	3	3
Vermont	3	8
New Hampshire	2	5
North Carolina	0	2
Rhode Island	0	8
Iowa	0	1
Maine	0	3
Kentucky	0	2
Virginia	25	25
South Carolina	6	0
Delaware	4	4
Massachusetts	0	3
FOREIGN COUNTRIES		
Canada	0	9
Ireland	1	0
England	5	0
Switzerland	1	0
Belgium	1	0
Prussia	1	0
Bavaria	2	0
Total	703	414

*These townships wholly within the example areas.
†This was the date of the first census in which the place of birth of persons was
recorded; from microfilm records of manuscript materials.

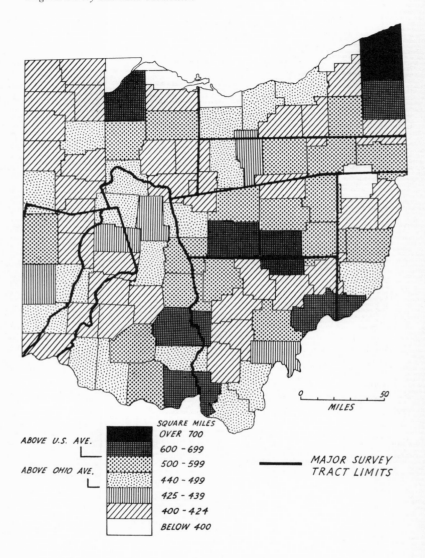

Appendix E Map of Counties of Ohio Showing Size (1955) and Major Survey Tracts. Note the general lack of agreement between the limits of major survey tracts and county boundaries as the latter are now constituted. There is no direct relationship between county size and major survey tracts.

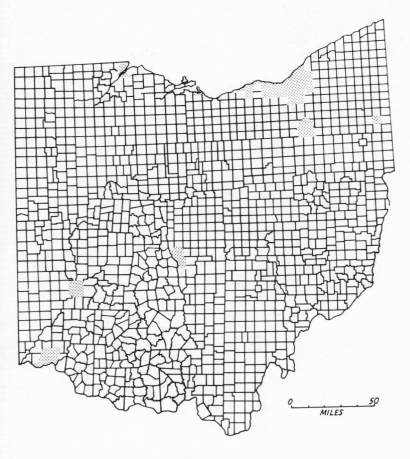

—— *CIVIL TOWNSHIP BOUNDARIES*

▒▒▒ *MAJOR URBAN AREAS*

Appendix F Map of Minor Civil Divisions (Civil Townships) Ohio, 1955. Note how the major survey tracts of Ohio are to some extent discernible in the pattern of civil townships, i.e., rectangular five-mile townships prevail in the Western Reserve and the United States Military Tracts. Elsewhere, six-mile townships predominate except in the Virginia Military District, where civil townships are highly variable as to shape and size. (From the map of Minor Civil Divisions, Bureau of the Census, United States Department of Commerce.)

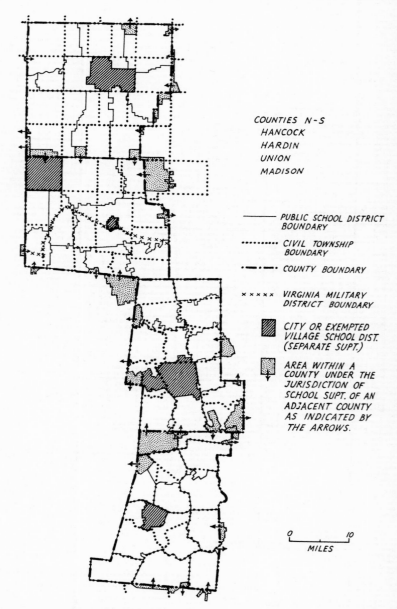

Appendix G Map of Public School Districts in a Four-County Area of Ohio (*c.* 1955). This map covers many times the area of examples S and U but embraces almost all of the area of these examples. It gives an overview of the complex relationships existing between educational and other administrative boundaries in Ohio. School districts compiled from manuscript maps in the offices of local school superintendents.

SELECTED BIBLIOGRAPHY

IN THE PREPARATION of this study various manuscript materials were examined and used, including items in government and nongovernment archives. In the office of the Auditor of State, Columbus, Ohio, appropriate field notes of original surveys, tract and sales entry books, surveyors contracts, as well as Canal and Indian Land documents were consulted and copied. Other manuscript materials utilized, and which are in the archives of the six counties particularly involved in this study, include maps and deed books related to local properties, roads, and railroads. Enumerated below are the main published sources used in this work, including the references cited, as well as maps not contained in the books, reports, and atlases listed.

Abernethy, Thomas P. *Western Lands and the American Revolution.* New York: D. Appleton-Century Company, 1937.

Adams, Herbert B. *Maryland's Influence Upon the Land Cessions to the United States.* Johns Hopkins University Studies in Historical and Political Science, Third Series, No. 1. Baltimore: Johns Hopkins University Press, 1885.

Allen County, Ohio: Office of the County Engineer. Copies of original cadastral maps of Jackson and Richland Townships. Scale 4 inches to 1 mile (approx.), 1955.

American State Papers, Documents Legislative and Executive of the Congress of the United States. Public Lands. Vol. 1-8. Washington: Gales and Seaton, 1832-1861.

Aumann, Francis R., and Walker, Harvey. *The Government and Administration of Ohio.* New York: Thomas Y. Crowell Company, 1956.

Barnes, Carlton P. "Economies of the Long Lot Farm," *Geographical Review,* 25 (April, 1935), 298-301.

Barnhart, John D. "The Southern Influence in the Formation of Ohio," *Journal of Southern History,* 3 (February, 1937), 28-48.

Binns, Sir Bernard O. *Cadastral Surveys and Records of Rights in Land.* Rome: Food and Agricultural Organization of the United Nations Agricultural Studies No. 18, 1953.

Bond, Beverley W., Jr. *The Civilization of the Old Northwest: A Study of Political, Social, and Economic Development, 1788-1812.* New York: The Macmillan Company, 1934.

Bradford, John. *Ancient Landscapes: Studies in Field Archaeology.* London: G. Bell and Sons, 1957.

Brown, C. R. *History of Hancock County, Ohio.* Chicago: Warner, Beers and Company, 1886.

Brown, Ralph H. *Historical Geography of the United States.* New York: Harcourt, Brace and Company, 1948.

————, *Mirror for Americans: Likeness of the Eastern Seaboard, 1810.* New York: American Geographical Society, 1943.

Bryan, Chester E. *History of Madison County, Ohio.* Indianapolis: Bowen and Company, 1915.

Buley, R. Carlyle. *The Old Northwest: Pioneer Period 1815-1840.* Vols 1-2. Indianapolis: Indiana Historical Society, 1950.

Caetani, Don Gelasio. "The 'Groma' or Cross Bar of the Roman Survey." *Engineering and Mining Journal-Press,* 118, No. 22 (November 29, 1924), 855.

Carstensen, Vernon (editor). *The Public Lands: Studies in the History of the Public Domain.* Madison, Wis.: The University of Wisconsin Press, 1963.

Chaddock, Robert E. *Ohio Before 1850: A Study of the Early Influence of Pennsylvania and Southern Populations in Ohio.* Columbia University Studies in History, Economics and Public Law, Vol. 31, No. 2. New York: Columbia University Press, 1908.

Champaign County, Ohio: Office of the County Engineer. Copies of original cadastral maps of Goshen and Rush Townships. Scale 4 inches to 1 mile (approx.), 1955.

Chandler, Alfred N. *Land Title Origins: A Tale of Force and Fraud.* New York: Robert Schalkenbach Foundation, 1945.

Christie, William D. *A Life of Anthony Ashley Cooper, First Earl of Shaftesbury, 1621-1683.* London: Macmillan and Company, 1871.

Copp, Henry N. *The American Settler's Guide: A Brief Exposition of the Public Land System of the United States.* Washington, D.C.: Henry N. Copp, 1880.

Cring, Henry. *Caldwell's Atlas of Madison County, Ohio.* Condit, Ohio: J. A. Caldwell, 1875.

Curry, William L. *History of Union County, Ohio.* Indianapolis: Bowen and Company, 1915.

Donaldson, Thomas. *The Public Domain: Its History with Statistics* (3rd edition). Washington, D.C.: Government Printing Office, 1884.

Downes, Randolph C. "Evolution of Ohio County Boundaries," *Ohio Archaeological and Historical Quarterly,* 36 (1927), 341-477.

Eberhart, G. A., and Pearce, C. J. *Illustrated Historical Atlas of Hancock County, Ohio.* Chicago: H. H. Hardesty, 1875.

Egleston, Melville. *The Land System of the New England Colonies.* Johns Hopkins University Studies in Historical and Political Science, Fourth Series, 11-12. Baltimore: Johns Hopkins University Press, 1886.

Elliot, Byron K., and Elliot, William F. *The Laws of Roads and Streets* (4th edition), Vol. 1. Indianapolis: The Bobbs-Merrill Company, 1926.

Fenneman, Nevin M. *The Physiography of the Eastern United States.* New York: McGraw-Hill Company, 1938.

Ford, Amelia C. *Colonial Precedents of Our National Land System, As It Existed in 1800.* Bulletin of the University of Wisconsin No. 352, History Series, Vol. 2, No. 2. Madison: University of Wisconsin Press, 1910.

Garland, John H. (editor). *The American Midwest: A Regional Geography.* New York: John Wiley and Sons, Inc., 1955.

Giauque, Florien. *The Laws Relating to Roads and Ditches, Bridges, and Water Courses in the State of Ohio.* Cincinnati: Robert Clark and Company, 1886.

Hancock County, Ohio: Office of the County Engineer. Copies of original cadastral maps of Eagle, Orange, Madison, Van Buren, and Union Townships. Scale 4 inches to 1 mile (approx.), 1955.

Hardin County, Ohio: Office of the County Engineer. Copies of original cadastral maps of Liberty and Washington Townships. Scale 4 inches to 1 mile (approx.), 1955.

Harris, Marshall. *Origin of the Land Tenure System in the United States.* Ames, Iowa: The Iowa State College Press, 1953.

Harrison, Robert H. *Atlas of Allen County, Ohio.* Philadelphia: R. H. Harrison, 1880.

Havighurst, Walter. *Wilderness for Sale: The Story of the First Western Land Rush.* New York: Hastings House, 1956.

Hening, William W. (editor). *The Statutes at Large: Being a Collection of All the Laws of Virginia,* Vol. 1. New York: R. and W. and G. Barton, 1823.

Hibbard, Benjamin H. *A History of the Public Land Policies.* New York: The Macmillan Company, 1924.

Higgins, Jerome S. *Subdivisions of the Public Lands.* Saint Louis, Mo.: Higgins and Co., 1887.

Hough, B., and Bourne, A. *Map of the State of Ohio from Actual Surveys.* Scale 1 inch to 5 miles (approx.). Philadelphia: B. Hough, A. Bourne and J. Melish, 1815.

Howland, H. G. *Atlas of Hardin County, Ohio.* Philadelphia: R. Sutton and Co., 1879.

Hulbert, Archer B. *Paths of the Mound-Building Indians and Great Game Animals: Historic Highways of America,* Vol. 1. Cleveland, Ohio: Arthur H. Clark Company, 1902.

Hutchinson, William T. *The Bounty Lands of the American Revolution in Ohio*. Unpublished Ph.D. dissertation, University of Chicago, 1927.

James, Preston E., and Jones, Clarence F. (editors). *American Geography, Inventory and Prospect*. Syracuse, N.Y.: Syracuse University Press, for the Association of American Geographers, 1954.

Jenny, George F. *Handbook to Aid in the Study of State and Local History (Ohio)*. Columbus, Ohio: Ohio Sesquicentennial Commission, 1953.

Jensen, Merrill. "The Cession of the Old Northwest," *Mississippi Valley Historical Review*, 23, No. 1 (June, 1936), 27-48.

––––––. "The Creation of the National Domain," *Mississippi Valley Historical Review*, 26, No. 3 (December, 1939), 323-342.

Johnson, Frank M. *The Rectangular System of Surveying*, in the United States Department of the Interior, *Public Land System of the United States*. Washington, D.C.: Government Printing Office, 1924.

Johnson, Hildegarde Binder. "Rational and Ecological Aspects of the Quarter Section: An Example from Minnesota," *Geographical Review*, 47 (July, 1957), 330-348.

Jones, Charles C., Jr. *The History of Georgia*, Vol. 1. Boston: Houghton Mifflin and Company, 1883.

Journals of the American Congress from 1774 to 1788, 4 vols. Washington, D.C.: Way and Gideon, 1823.

Kish, George. "Centuriatio: The Roman Rectangular Land Survey," *Surveying and Mapping*, 22, No. 2 (June, 1962), 233-244.

Kniffen, Fred. "To Know the Land and Its People," *Landscape*, 9, No. 3 (Spring, 1960), 20-23.

Knight, George W. "History of Educational Progress in Ohio," in *Historical Collections of Ohio*, Henry Howe (editor), Vol. 1. Cincinnati, Ohio: C. J. Krehbiel and Company, 1902.

Laning, Jay F. "The Evolution of Ohio Counties," *Ohio Archaeological and Historical Society Publications*, 5 (1897), 326-350.

Larcom, Sir Thomas A. (editor). *The History of the Down Survey of Doctor William Petty*. Dublin: The Irish Archaeological Society, 1851.

Le Gear, Clara E. *United States Atlases*, Vols. 1-2. Washington, D.C.: The Library of Congress, 1950, 1953.

Madison County, Ohio: Office of the County Engineer. Copies of original cadastral maps of Pike and Summerford Townships. Scale 4 inches to 1 mile (approx.), 1955.

Marschner, Francis J. *Boundaries and Records in the Territory of Early Settlement from Canada to Florida, with Historical Notes on the Cadaster and Its Potential Value in the Area*. Washington, D.C.: Agricultural Research Service, United States Department of Agriculture, 1960.

––––––. *Land Use and Its Patterns in the United States: Agricultural Handbook No. 153*. Washington, D.C.: United States Department of Agriculture, 1959.

Marshall, Sir John H. *Mohenjo-Daro and the Indus Civilization*, Vol. 1. London: Arthur Probsthian, 1931.

McGraw-Hill Encyclopedia of Science and Technology, Vol. 13. New York: McGraw-Hill Book Company, 1960.

Miller, Edward A. "History of the Educational Legislation in Ohio from 1803 to 1850," *Ohio Archaeological and Historical Publications,* 27 (1919), 1-271.

Mills, William C. *Archaeological Atlas of Ohio.* Columbus, Ohio: Ohio State Archaeological and Historical Publications, 1914.

Mowry, Andrew S. *Atlas of Union County, Ohio.* Philadelphia: Harrison, Sutton, and Hare, 1877.

Munzenmayer, Lester H., and Morgan, T. O. *A Handbook for Members of Boards of Education in Ohio.* Columbus: State of Ohio, Department of Education, 1946.

Ohio, State. *A Compilation of Laws, Treaties, Resolutions and Ordinances of the General and State Government Which Relate to Lands in the State of Ohio.* Columbus: G. Nashee, 1825.

_____. *Acts Passed at the First Session of the 18th General Assembly Begun and Held at Columbus, December, 1819,* Vol. 18. Columbus: Office of the Columbus Gazette, 1820.

_____. *A Short History of Ohio Land Grants.* Columbus: Office of the Auditor of State, 1955.

_____. Department of Education. *Educational Directory of the State of Ohio, 1955-1956.* Compiled by Morna R. Larrick. Columbus: F. J. Heer, 1955.

_____. Department of Highways. *Classification by Surface Type of Existing Mileage in Each County on State Highway, County and Township Systems.* Columbus: Bureau of Planning Survey, 1956. (mimeographed).

_____. Department of Highways, County Highway Maps: Allen (1952); Champaign (1940); Fayette (1953); Hardin (1952); Hancock (1941); Madison (1953); Marion (1953); Union (1953); Wyandot (1951). Scale, 1:125,000 (approx.).

_____. Department of Highways. *Map of the State Highway System (1954).* Scale, 1:750,000.

_____. Department of Highways. *Ohio Highway Laws.* Cleveland, Ohio: Banks-Baldwin Law Publishing Company, 1954.

_____. Department of Highways. *Ohio Highway Laws: Supplement to the 1954 Edition.* Cleveland, Ohio: Banks-Baldwin Law Publishing Company, 1956.

_____. Department of Highways. *Traffic Flow Map of Ohio (1952).* Scale, 1:750,000 (approx.).

_____. Department of Natural Resources. *Mineral Industry Map (1953).* Scale, 1:500,000.

_____. Department of Natural Resources. *Principal Streams and Drainage Areas.* Map (1953). Scale, 1:800,000.

_____. Department of Public Works, Geological Survey of Ohio. *Geological Map of Ohio,* compiled by J. A. Bownocker (1947). Scale, 1:500,000.

————. Development and Publicity Commission. *Ohio, An Empire Within an Empire* (2nd edition). Guy-Harold Smith (editor). Columbus 1950.

Overman, William D. *Select List of Materials on Ohio History in Serial Publications.* Columbus: Ohio State Archaeological and Historical Society, 1941.

Pattison, William D. *Beginnings of the American Rectangular Land Survey System, 1784-1800.* A Dissertation Submitted to the Faculty of the Division of the Social Sciences, University of Chicago. Department of Geography Research Paper, No. 50. Chicago: University of Chicago Press, 1957.

————. "The Original Plan Behind the Rectangular Subdivision of Land in the Old Northwest," *Annals of the Association of American Geographers,* 47, No. 2 (June, 1957), 174.

————. "The Original Plan for an American Rectangular Land Survey," *Surveying and Mapping,* 21, No. 3 (1961), 339-345.

Paullin, Charles O. *Atlas of the Historical Geograph of the United States,* John K. Wright, editor. Washington, D.C.: Carnegie Institution of Washingon and the American Geographical Society, 1932.

Peters, William E. *Ohio Lands and Their Subdivision* (2nd edition). Athens, Ohio: W. E. Peters, 1918.

Phillips, Philip L. *A List of Geographical Atlases in the Library of Congress.* Vols. 1-4. Washington, D.C.: Government Printing Office, 1909-1920.

Prendergast, John P. *The Cromwellian Settlement of Ireland* (2nd edition). Dublin: McGlashan and Gill, 1875.

Prunty, Merle, Jr. "The Renaissance of the Southern Plantation," *Geographical Review,* 45 (October, 1955), 459-491.

Robbins, Roy M. *Our Landed Heritage: The Public Domain 1776-1936.* Princeton: Princeton University Press, 1942.

Rose, Albert H. *Ohio Government, State and Local,* Ohio Sesquicentennial Edition. Saint Louis, Mo.: Educational Publishers, Inc., 1953.

Roseboom, Eugene H., and Weisenburger, Francis P. *A History of Ohio.* New York: Prentice-Hall, Inc., 1934.

Sato, Shosuke. *History of the Land Question in the United States.* Johns Hopkins University Studies in Historical and Political Science, Fourth Series Nos. 7, 8, 9. Baltimore: Johns Hopkins University Press, 1886.

Sears, Alfred B. *Thomas Worthington: Father of Ohio Statehood.* Columbus: Ohio State University Press, for the Ohio Historical Society, 1958.

Sears, Paul B. "The Natural Vegetation of Ohio; I, Map of the Virgin Forest," *The Ohio Journal of Science,* 25, No. 3 (May, 1925), 139-149.

————. "The Natural Vegetation of Ohio; II, The Prairies," *The Ohio Journal of Science,* 26, No. 3 (May, 1926), 128-146.

Shanks, Royal E. "Forest Composition and Species Association of the Beech-Maple Forest Region of Western Ohio," *Ecology*, 34, No. 3 (July, 1953), 455-466.

Sherman, C. E. *Original Ohio Land Subdivisions*. Vol. III of four volumes. Columbus: Final Report, Ohio Cooperative Topographic Survey, 1925.

Smith, Dwight L. "Nine Letters of Nathaniel Dike on the Western Country, 1816-1818," *The Ohio Historical Quarterly*, 67, No. 3 (July, 1958), 189-220.

Smith, Guy-Harold. "A Population Map of Ohio for 1920," *Geographical Review*, 18 (July, 1928), 422-427.

_____. "The Relative Relief of Ohio," *Geographical Review*, 25 (April, 1935), 272-284.

Smith, William. *Historical Account of Bouquet's Expedition Against the Ohio Indians, in 1764*. Cincinnati: Robert Clarke and Company, 1868.

Starr, J. W., and Headington, J. N. *Atlas of Champaign County, Ohio*. Urbana, Ohio: Starr and Headington, 1874.

Thomson, Peter G. *A Bibliography of the State of Ohio*. Cincinnati: Peter G. Thomson, 1880.

Thornthwaite, C. Warren. "The Climates of North America According to a New Classification," *Geographical Review*, 21 (October, 1931), 633-655.

Thrower, Norman J. W. "Cadastral Survey and Roads in Ohio," *Annals of the Association of American Geographers*, 47, No. 2 (June, 1957), 181-182.

_____. "The County Atlas of the United States." *Surveying and Mapping*, 21, No. 3 (September, 1961), 365-373.

Treat, Payson J. *The National Land System, 1785-1820*. New York: E. B. Treat and Co., 1910.

Trewartha, Glenn T. *An Introduction to Climate*, (3rd edition). New York: McGraw-Hill Book Company, Inc., 1954.

Turner, Frederick J. "The Old West," *Proceedings of the State Historical Society of Wisconsin*. Madison, Wis.: State Historical Society of Wisconsin, 1908. Pp. 184-233.

Union County, Ohio: Office of the County Engineer. Copies of cadastral maps of Darby and Union Townships. Scale 4 inches to 1 mile (approx.), 1955.

United States Census. *The Seventh Census of the United States, 1850*. Washington, D.C.: Robert Armstrong, Printer, 1853.

United States, Department of Agriculture. *Atlas of American Agriculture*. Oliver E. Baker (editor). Part II, Section I, *Frost and the Growing Season*, by William G. Reed. Washington, D.C.: Government Printing Office, 1920.

————, Department of Agriculture. *Erosion Survey Map of Ohio.* Scale, 1:500,000. 1935.

————, Department of Agriculture. *Major Soils of the North-Central Region.* Map Publication No. 76, compiled by the States of the North-Central Region. Scale, 1:3,000,000. 1957.

————, Department of Commerce. *Ohio: Minor Civil Divisions-Townships.* Scale, 1:500,000 (approx.). 1941, 1951, 1961.

————, Department of Commerce, Bureau of the Census. *Areas of the United States (1940).* Washington, D.C.: Government Printing Office, 1942.

————, Department of Commerce, Bureau of the Census. *Census of Population; 1950,* Vol. 2, Part 35, Ohio. Washington, D.C.: Government Printing Office, 1952.

————, Department of Commerce, Bureau of the Census. *Census of Population PC (1)-37B, Ohio, 1960.* Washington, D.C.: Government Printing Office, 1961.

————, Department of Commerce, Bureau of Public Roads. *Ohio Transportation Map* (6 sheets). Scale, 1:250,000. 1949.

————, Department of the Interior. *Manual of Instructions for the Survey of the Public Lands of the United States, 1930.* Washington, D.C.: Government Printing Office, 1930.

————, Department of the Interior. *United States Showing Principal Meridians and Base Lines.* Map. Scale, 1:6,000,000. 1942.

————, Department of the Interior, Geological Survey. Topographic Maps (quadrangles), *Arlington; Bluffton; Mechanicsburg; Milford Center.* Scale, 1:62,500.

Utter, William T. *The Frontier State, 1803-1825,* Vol. 2, *The History of the State of Ohio* (in six volumes). Carl Wittke (editor). Columbus: Ohio State Archaeological and Historical Society, 1942.

Walling, Henry F., and Gray, Ormando W. *New Topographical Atlas of the State of Ohio.* Cincinnati: Stedman, Brown and Lyon, 1872.

Ward, David. "The Pre-Urban Cadaster and the Urban Pattern of Leeds," *Annals of the Association of American Geographers,* 52, No. 2 (June, 1962), 150-166.

Weaver, John C. "Crop-Combination Regions in the Middle West," *Geographical Review,* 44 (April, 1954), 175-200.

Wilgus, James A. "Evolution of Township Government in Ohio," *Annual Report of the American Historical Association for the Year 1894.* Washington, D.C.: Government Printing Office, 1895.

Wilson, Samuel M. *Catalogue of Revolutionary Soldiers and Sailors of the Commonwealth of Virginia.* Baltimore: Southern Book Company, 1953.

Wittke, Carl (Editor). *The History of the State of Ohio* (in six volumes). Columbus: Ohio State Archaeological and Historical Society, 1942.

Wright, Alfred J. *Economic Geography of Ohio* (2nd edition). Columbus: Ohio Department of Natural Resources, Division of Geological Survey Bulletin 50, 1957.

————. "Ohio Town Patterns," *Geographical Review,* 27 (October, 1937), 615-624.

INDEX

Upright numbers, without qualification, are used for textual references. The letter "n" indicates references to footnotes and precedes the page number on which the footnote appears. Page references to maps, graphs, tables, illustrations, and appendixes are in italics.